PADUA
TRAVEL GUIDE 2025

The Ultimate Insider's Guide and Maps to Italy's Hidden Jewel

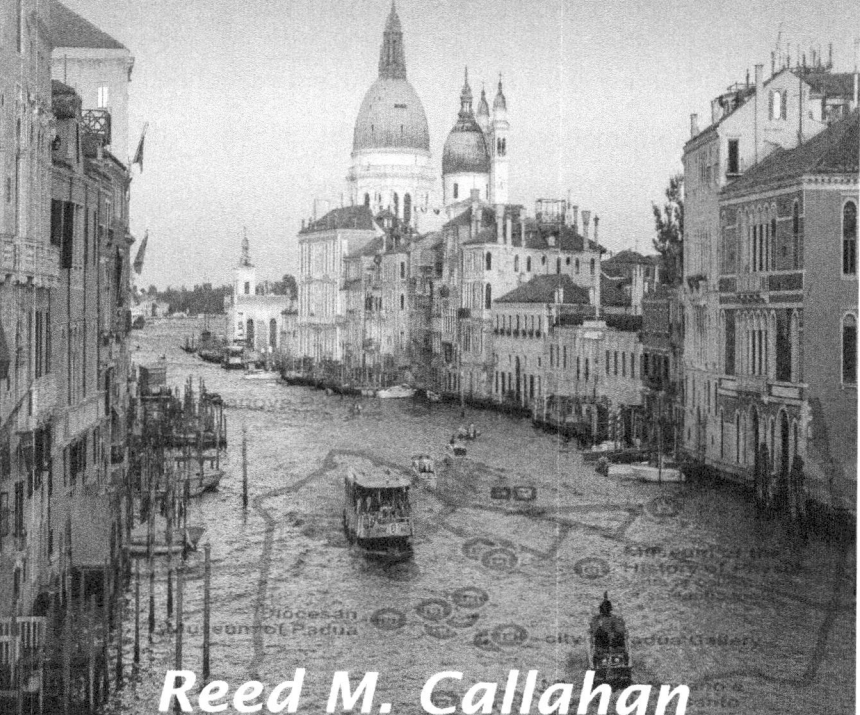

Reed M. Callahan

1

Table of Contents

Table of Contents 3

Introduction 7

    Life in Padua: The Daily Beat 9

    Famous Faces and Local Legends 10

    The Quirks and Challenges of Padua 10

    A Journey Through History 11

    Food That Captures the Essence of Veneto 12

    A Youthful Vibe and Authentic Italian Life 12

    A Gateway to Northern Italy..13

    Insider's Tip: Beyond the Obvious................................13

    How to Use This Guide 14

Chapter 1: Getting to Padua 17

    By Air: Nearest Airports..17

    By Train: Routes from Major Cities (Venice, Milan, Bologna) 20

    By Car: Road Routes and Parking in Padua....................21

    Public Transport Options in Padua................................23

Chapter 2: Top Attractions in Padua 25

    Scrovegni Chapel: A Masterpiece of Early Renaissance Art............26

    Basilica of Saint Anthony: A Pilgrim's Dream 27

    Prato della Valle: Europe's Largest Square 28

Palazzo della Ragione: A Medieval Masterpiece 29

University of Padua: A Hub of Knowledge...........................30

Orto Botanico: A Green Oasis 31

Chapter 3: Art and Museums in Padua *33*

Museo Civico agli Eremitani: Archaeology and Renaissance Art 33

Museo del Precinema: A Window into the Birth of Film.................35

Temporary Exhibitions: Contemporary Art in Padua 37

Chapter 4: Exploring Padua's Religious Heritage *39*

Religious Pilgrimages and Sites of Interest...........................40

Spiritual Journey Through the City...........................41

Oratory of San Giorgio: A Hidden Gem 42

Local Religious Festivals: The Saint Anthony Festival 43

Sacred Etiquette: Tips for Visiting Religious Sites 44

Chapter 5: Dining in Padua: A Feast for the Senses *47*

Must-Try Dishes and Local Specialties...........................47

Best Restaurants, Trattorias, and Osterias 49

Wine and Dine: Veneto's Best Wines 50

Chapter 6: Local Food Markets *53*

The Soul of Padua's Culinary Scene...........................53

Artisan Souvenirs: Pottery, Ceramics, and Handcrafted Goods 56

How to Identify Authentic Artisanal Products...........................57

Best Markets for Shopping: Weekly Markets at Piazza dei Signori .58

Chapter 7: Parks and Outdoor Spaces in Padua *61*

Nature and History Intertwined...........................61

Prato della Valle: A Green Escape in the City.......................61

Orto Botanico: Discovering Botanical Wonders...................63

Walking and Biking Trails Along Padua's Canals 65

Chapter 8: Local Festivals and Events in Padua *69*

A Celebration of Tradition, Taste, and Talent.....................69

Saint Anthony Festival: Religious Processions and Celebrations.....69

Food and Wine Festivals: The Best of Padua's Culinary Traditions .71

Music and Theatre Performances: Opera and Classical Concerts 73

Chapter 9: Nightlife and Entertainment in Padua.............*77*

From Evening Hangouts to Live Performances 77

Evening Hangouts: Piazza delle Erbe and Piazza della Frutta 77

Best Bars and Cafes for a Night Out 79

Live Music Venues and Theatre Performances 81

Chapter 10: Day Trips from Padua *85*

Discovering the Veneto Region 85

Venice: The Perfect Day Trip...85

Exploring the Euganean Hills...88

Vicenza and Verona 90

Chapter 11: Practical Information for Travelers Visiting Padua .93

Best Time to Visit Padua: Weather Guide 93

Public Transportation: Trams, Buses, and Bicycle Rentals 95

Tourist Passes: The Padova Card....................................97

Understanding Local Customs and Etiquette..................99

Chapter 12: Hidden Gems of Padua.........................*103*

Uncovering the City's Lesser-Known Treasures 103

Jewish Ghetto: A Quiet Piece of History..................................103

Roman Ruins: Discovering Padua's Ancient Past 105

Lesser-Known Churches and Chapels: Spiritual Treasures Off the Beaten Path..107

Chapter 13: Safety, Health, and Travel Tips for Visitors to Padua *111*

Health and Safety: Emergency Contacts and Tips........................111

Travel Insurance and Health Services....................................114

The Healthcare System in Padua..115

Currency and Tipping Etiquette in Italy 121

Conclusion *124*

Map of Padua.. *131*

Map of Cheap Hotels in Padua...132

Map of Where to Stay in Padua 133

Map of Where to Eat in Padua 134

Map of Beaches near Padua 135

Map of Museums in Padua 136

Map of where to Hike in and Around Padua 137

Map of Padua's Historic sites..138

Map of Padua's Best Shopping Spots 139

Map of Public Transportation in Padua....................................140

Map of Parks and Gardens in Padua 141

Introduction

Welcome to Padua, Italy – a city where history, art, and academic brilliance create an unforgettable experience. Nestled in the heart of the Veneto region, Padua often flies under the radar of travelers rushing between its famous neighbors, Venice and Verona. But those who pause to explore quickly discover that Padua, with its rich history, vibrant culture, and modern charm, has a unique personality.

Just 40 kilometers west of Venice, Padua's strategic location makes it a convenient stop for those venturing across northern Italy. It's a place where the past feels tangible, with medieval streets winding past ancient buildings and bustling piazzas alive with locals sipping espresso. Yet, it also pulses with the energy of a modern university town, home to one of Europe's oldest universities. It has helped shape the city into an intellectual and cultural hub for nearly 800 years.

A City Steeped in History and Art

Padua's story dates back to pre-Roman times but flourished in the Middle Ages and the Renaissance. Known as **Padova** in Italian, the city became a key center of learning, art, and commerce. Its intellectual prowess is best exemplified by the **University of Padua**, founded in 1222, where Galileo Galilei lectured in the 16th century. Walking through the university's ancient courtyards, you can almost feel the echoes of scholarly debates that have shaped science and philosophy for centuries.

One of Padua's most awe-inspiring gems is the **Scrovegni Chapel**, often hailed as one of the most outstanding artistic achievements of the early Renaissance. Giotto's vivid frescoes, which cover the walls and ceiling, bring the stories of Christ and Mary to life in breathtaking detail. The colors and expressions are so fresh that it's hard to believe they were painted over 700 years ago. Be sure to book your visit in advance – the chapel's strict climate control allows only a limited number of visitors at a time, preserving this masterpiece for future generations.

The Soul of Padua

Despite its historical weight, Padua feels refreshingly youthful. This is primarily thanks to the thriving student population, which infuses the city with a lively, modern vibe. Wander through Prato della Valle, one of Europe's largest squares, and you'll see a perfect blend of life's rhythms. Joggers and cyclists weave through the paths, students study under trees, and locals chat by the many statues that encircle the square. It's a peaceful place that offers relaxation and a sense of connection to the city's storied past.

The Basilica of Saint Anthony, a towering pilgrimage site, symbolizes the city's deep religious roots. Known affectionately by locals as "Il Santo," it's one of Italy's most visited churches. Even if you're not religious, the atmosphere inside is undeniably moving.

The basilica also houses Saint Anthony's relics, and its grand architecture is worth admiring, both for its scale and intricate details.

Life in Padua: The Daily Beat

While Padua's attractions draw tourists from around the globe, it remains a city grounded in daily life. The Piazza delle Erbe and Piazza della Frutta are lively squares where you can experience Padua's bustling market scene. These markets have been around since medieval times, and today, they remain the heart of local life. Here, you can grab fresh produce, sample cheeses, or soak up the atmosphere over a cappuccino as vendors call out to shoppers in melodic Italian.

Speaking of food, Padua is a city that knows how to eat. From traditional trattorias serving up risotto alla Padovana to modern eateries experimenting with the flavors of Veneto, the city's culinary scene offers something for everyone. Don't forget to pair your meal with a glass of local Prosecco or Soave, which hail from vineyards just outside the city.

Famous Faces and Local Legends

Padua's influence extends far beyond its city limits. Galileo is just one of the many famous names associated with Padua. The university's alumni list reads like a who's who of great thinkers, including Copernicus and Andrea Vesalius, the father of modern anatomy. Padua's Anatomical Theatre, the world's first permanent structure built to study human dissection, still stands as a testament to the city's pioneering spirit in medicine and science.

Local legends also whisper that a mysterious "golden goose" is said to bring good fortune to those who find it hidden within the city. Whether this tale is accurate or not, Padua certainly feels like a treasure waiting to be uncovered by the curious traveler.

The Quirks and Challenges of Padua

Like every city, Padua has its quirks. While its charm lies in its walkable, medieval streets, these narrow alleys can occasionally frustrate those unused to navigating them. The weather, too, can be unpredictable – warm and inviting one minute, with sudden rain showers the next. But these small challenges only add to the city's authentic feel, reminding you that Padua is a place where history and modern life coexist, sometimes messily, but always beautifully.

A City Waiting to Be Discovered

Padua might have a different name recognition than Venice or Florence, but that makes it so unique. It's a city where you can wander without crowds, where every turn reveals a new layer of history or a hidden piazza. Whether you're an art lover, a history buff, or just someone looking for an authentic Italian experience, Padua has something to offer. Ready to explore? Let's dive into everything this remarkable city has in store.

Why Visit Padua?

Suppose you've ever dreamed of walking through a city where history, art, and science seem to echo from every cobblestone. In that case, Padua is the destination you've been waiting for. Often overshadowed by nearby Venice, Padua (or Padova, as it's known in Italian) is a hidden gem that surprises and delights those who take the time to explore its winding streets and lively piazzas. Here's why this captivating city should top your travel list.

A Journey Through History

One of the most compelling reasons to visit Padua is its rich historical and cultural significance. This is, after all, the city that gave birth to one of the world's oldest universities, the University of Padua, founded in 1222. This institution has shaped the course of European intellectual history. It boasts a roster of famous scholars, including the legendary Galileo Galilei. Imagine standing in the same university halls where Galileo once taught, gazing up at the stars and pondering the mysteries of the universe. Padua's academic heritage is not just history on display—it's a living, breathing part of the city's vibrant identity today.

Art That Takes Your Breath Away

Padua is home to one of the world's most extraordinary pieces of art: Giotto's frescoes in the Scrovegni Chapel. These stunning works, created in the early 14th century, are often regarded as the spark that ignited the Italian Renaissance. As you stand beneath the chapel's brilliantly blue ceiling, you'll feel like you've stepped into a sacred space where time pauses. Each fresco tells a story, from Christ's life to everyday medieval life scenes, and the vivid colors and expressions are so fresh that it's hard to believe they've survived for centuries. Visiting the Scrovegni Chapel is a must for any art lover, but be sure to book in advance—access is tightly controlled to preserve this masterpiece.

The City That Shaped Science

Padua isn't just about art; it's also a city where science and medicine flourished. The University of Padua's Anatomical Theatre, the first of its kind, is where early pioneers of medicine dissected cadavers to advance human understanding of the body. It's a thrilling—and slightly eerie—place that offers a glimpse into the city's role in shaping modern science. Visitors can still explore this unique venue, where seats rise steeply around a small stage, once filled with students eager to learn about the mysteries of human anatomy. This connection between Padua and scientific discovery continues to draw those interested in history, medicine, and the progress of human knowledge.

Food That Captures the Essence of Veneto

Every trip to Padua would be complete with diving into its culinary treasures. The city sits in the heart of the Veneto region, known for its hearty, flavorful dishes and world-class wines. Local specialties like bigoli in salsa, a thick spaghetti-like pasta served with a rich sauce, or risotto alla Padovana, a creamy risotto made with peas and local herbs, will have your taste buds dancing. And let's not forget the wine—Proseccolovers will find themselves in paradise here, with vineyards just a short drive away. Whether dining in a rustic trattoria or exploring the bustling markets of Piazza delle Erbe, Padua's food scene offers an authentic taste of Northern Italy that's hard to beat.

A Youthful Vibe and Authentic Italian Life

What makes Padua incredibly unique is its **vibrant atmosphere**. Thanks to its thriving student population, the city feels youthful and energetic. Yet, it retains a relaxed pace that invites you to slow down and enjoy life. Stroll through the **Prato della Valle**, Europe's largest square, and you'll see locals chatting over coffee, students sprawled out with books, and joggers circling its grand fountains and statues. The pace of daily life here offers an authentic glimpse into Italian culture without the tourist crowds that often overwhelm cities like Florence or Rome.

A Gateway to Northern Italy

Convenience is another reason Padua deserves a place on your itinerary. Located just 30 minutes by train from Venice, Padua is the perfect base for exploring Northern Italy. With its excellent transport connections, you can easily take day trips to Venice, Verona, or even the beautiful Euganean Hills, where thermal spas and vineyards await. Yet, unlike Venice, Padua has retained its distinctly Italian character, allowing travelers to enjoy an authentic experience without the inflated prices and crowded streets.

Insider's Tip: Beyond the Obvious

Padua has its hidden gems, too. Walk through the **Jewish Ghetto**, where narrow streets and quiet courtyards reveal a fascinating layer of the city's history. Or explore the **Orto Botanico**, the world's oldest university botanical garden, a peaceful retreat where plants from around the world flourish. And if you're looking for a quirky local tradition, keep your eye out for the legend of the **Golden Goose**, which is said to bring good luck to those who find it hidden in the city.

Why Not Just a Day Trip?

Many travelers assume Padua is a quick stopover on the way to Venice. Still, nothing could be further from the truth. Sure, you can visit in a day, but Padua is a city that rewards those who linger. Whether savoring the local food, wandering through historic streets, or soaking up the academic atmosphere, Padua has a charm that deserves more than a rushed afternoon.

Padua is not just a city to visit—it's a city to experience, and once you do, it will leave an indelible mark on your soul. Whether you're drawn by its art, history, food, or vibrant street life, Padua offers a perfect blend of the past and present, with something new to discover around every corner. So pack your bags, bring your curiosity, and get ready to fall in love with this hidden gem of Northern Italy.

How to Use This Guide

Welcome to Padua! Whether you're here for a quick day trip or an extended stay, this guide will help you get the most out of visiting this beautiful and historic city. Our goal is simple: to make sure you experience the best Padua, from its must-see landmarks to the hidden gems only locals know about.

The guide is structured to be both comprehensive and easy to use, so no matter how you like to travel, we've got you covered. Here's what you'll find inside:

- **Overview of Padua**: Start here for a big-picture introduction to the city, its vibe, and what makes it so unique.
- **Historical Background**: Curious about Padua's fascinating past? This section gives you the highlights, from ancient Roman roots to its role in the Renaissance.
- **Main Attractions**: Your go-to list for the top sights, like the stunning Scrovegni Chapel and the Basilica of Saint Anthony.
- **Off-the-Beaten-Path Experiences**: Want to explore beyond the crowds? Discover unique spots and local secrets here.
- **Food and Drink**: All the info you need to eat like a local, from traditional trattorias to the best places for Prosecco.
- **Accommodation Options**: Whether on a budget or looking for something special, this section helps you find the perfect place to rest your head.

- **Practical Information**: Tips on transportation, safety, and everything else you need to know to navigate the city like a pro.

How to Use the Guide

We've included several handy features to make things as easy as possible. If you're short on time, **use the Table of Contents or Index to** find precisely what you want. Throughout the book, keep an eye out for symbols:
- ★ **Must-See**: Don't miss these iconic sights!
- 💡 **Insider Tip**: Local advice to enhance your experience.

Whether you're planning a **day trip** or a more extended stay, we've organized the guide to suit your style. Head straight to the **Main Attractions** section for day-trippers and hit the highlights. If you're staying longer, explore the **Off-the-Beaten-Path** experiences for a deeper dive into Padua's local charm.

Are you traveling for art, history, or food? Flip to the sections that interest you most, or use our **customizable itineraries to** plan your ideal day. And yes, there's even a little something for the indecisive—we've got suggested routes to help guide your journey.

A Friendly Warning

Now, we should warn you: there's a real danger you'll fall in love with Padua and want to stay longer than planned. So, don't be surprised if one day turns into two… or more! After all, this city has a way of stealing hearts.

With that said, you're all set to dive in. Let's start exploring the wonders of Padua together. **Andiamo a Padova!**

Chapter 1: Getting to Padua

Whether flying in from afar, taking a train through Italy's scenic routes, or hitting the open road, Padua is easy to reach. As a well-connected city in the Veneto region, Padua offers various transportation options that suit every type of traveler. This guide will walk you through everything you need to know about getting to Padua, from the nearest airports to train routes, driving tips, and public transportation once you've arrived.

By Air: Nearest Airports

When flying into Padua, your nearest options are Venice Marco Polo Airport (VCE), Treviso Antonio Canova Airport (TSF), and Bologna Guglielmo Marconi Airport (BLQ). Each offers a range of airlines and easy connections to Padua.

1. **Venice Marco Polo Airport (VCE)**

   - **Distance to Padua**: 45 kilometers (28 miles)
   - **Travel Time to Padua**: 40-60 minutes by car or bus, 1-1.5 hours by train
   - **Airlines**: Major international carriers like Lufthansa, British Airways, Air France, Emirates, and low-cost airlines such as Ryanair and EasyJet.
   - **Getting to Padua**:
     - **By Bus**: The ATVO and BusItalia run direct buses from Marco Polo Airport to Padua's city center. The buses are comfortable, with air conditioning and luggage space. Tickets cost €8-10, and the journey takes approximately 1 hour.
     - **By Train**: Take a shuttle bus from the airport to **Venice Mestre** station (about 15 minutes, costing €8). Trains from Venice Mestre to Padua run frequently and take about 30 minutes, costing €4-12 depending on the train type.
     - **By Taxi or Private Transfer**: Taxis from Marco Polo Airport to Padua cost around €90-120, depending on traffic. Alternatively, you can pre-book a private transfer for convenience. Expect to pay more for this service, especially if you're traveling during peak hours.

Insider Tip: The direct bus is your best bet if you're in a rush and want to avoid train changes. The train offers scenic views for those wishing to catch the beautiful Venetian landscape.

2. **Treviso Antonio Canova Airport (TSF)**
   -
   - **Distance to Padua**: 60 kilometers (37 miles)

- **Travel Time to Padua**: 1-1.5 hours by car or bus, 1.5-2 hours by train
- **Airlines**: Mostly serviced by low-cost carriers like Ryanair and Wizz Air.
- **Getting to Padua**:
    - **By Bus**: Barzi Bus Service offers a direct connection from Treviso Airport to Padua for around €12, taking about 1 hour and 15 minutes.
    - **By Train**: Take a shuttle bus from Treviso Airport to **Treviso Centrale** station (about 15 minutes, costing €3). From there, catch a train to Padua, which takes around 1 hour. Ticket prices vary from €7-15, depending on the train type.
    - **By Taxi or Private Transfer**: A taxi ride from Treviso Airport to Padua will cost approximately €110-140, depending on the time of day.

Insider Tip: If you arrive late in the evening, check the last bus or train schedules in advance—public transport options taper off after 9 PM.

3. **Bologna Guglielmo Marconi Airport (BLQ)**
    -
    - **Distance to Padua**: 120 kilometers (75 miles)
    - **Travel Time to Padua**: 1.5-2 hours by car or train
    - **Airlines**: Serves major international carriers like KLM, Turkish Airlines, and Lufthansa, alongside budget airlines.
    - **Getting to Padua**:
        - **By Train**: Take the **Marconi Express** shuttle (€8.70, 7 minutes) from the airport to Bologna Centrale station. From there, high-speed trains to Padua take about 1 hour. Tickets range from €14-30.

- **By Bus**: A few long-distance buses connect Bologna Airport to Padua, taking around 2 hours. Tickets cost about €10-15.
- **By Taxi or Private Transfer**: Taxis from Bologna Airport to Padua cost around €180-220, depending on traffic and timing.

Insider Tip: For those flying internationally, Bologna Airport often has cheaper flights than Venice, especially during peak travel seasons. Plus, the train from Bologna Centrale is fast and convenient.

By Train: Routes from Major Cities (Venice, Milan, Bologna)

Padua is a major stop on Italy's high-speed train network, making it an easy destination for those traveling by rail. Whether you're coming from Venice, Milan, or Bologna, trains to Padua are frequent, efficient, and comfortable.

1. **Venice to Padua**

- **Distance**: 40 kilometers (25 miles)
- **Journey Time**: 30-45 minutes
- **Train Types**: Both high-speed trains (Frecciarossa, Italo) and regional trains (Regionale Veloce) run frequently.
- **Ticket Cost**: €4-25, depending on train type. Regional trains are the cheapest, while high-speed trains are faster and more expensive.
- **Frequency**: Trains depart Venice for Padua every 15-30 minutes.
- **Booking Tips**: Tickets can be purchased at the station or online through websites like **Trenitalia** or **Italo**. For high-speed trains, booking in advance can save you up to 50%.

2. **Milan to Padua**

-
- **Distance**: 240 kilometers (150 miles)
- **Journey Time**: 2-2.5 hours
- **Train Types**: High-speed trains (Frecciarossa, Italo) dominate this route, but slower intercity options are also available.
- **Ticket Cost**: €25-60, depending on train type and booking time.
- **Frequency**: Trains depart roughly every hour.
- **Booking Tips**: Booking online in advance is highly recommended for savings and seat availability. For those in no rush, slower intercity trains are more affordable.

3. **Bologna to Padua**

- **Distance**: 120 kilometers (75 miles)
- **Journey Time**: 50 minutes to 1.5 hours
- **Train Types**: High-speed trains (Frecciarossa, Italo) are the fastest option, with some slower regional trains available.
- **Ticket Cost**: €12-30, depending on train type.
- **Frequency**: Trains depart every 30-45 minutes.
- **Booking Tips**: Regional trains are cheaper but slower, so consider your timing when choosing.

Padua Train Station

Padua's Stazione **di Padova** is centrally located and well-equipped with cafes, shops, ATMs, and luggage storage. From the station, the city's main attractions are just a short walk or a quick tram ride away. For a pre-departure espresso, grab a coffee at **Caffè Pedrocchi**, a historic cafe just a 10-minute walk from the station.

By Car: Road Routes and Parking in Padua

Driving to Padua offers flexibility and the opportunity to explore the surrounding Veneto countryside. Major highways make access easy, but there are a few things to keep in mind, including tolls and limited traffic zones (ZTL) in the city center.

1. **Major Road Routes to Padua**
    -
        - **From Venice**: Take the A57 highway and merge onto the A4 towards Padua. The drive is about 45 minutes.
        - **From Milan**: Follow the A4 motorway east toward Venice, passing through Bergamo and Verona. The drive takes about 2.5 hours.
        - **From Bologna**: Head north on the A13 motorway, and you'll reach Padua in roughly 1.5 hours.

2. **Toll Roads and Costs**

Italy's highways, or **autostrada**, are toll roads. You'll collect a ticket when you enter and pay based on distance traveled. For example, tolls from Milan to Padua are around €20, while Venice to Padua is about €5. Be sure to have cash or a credit card ready at the toll booths.

3. **Driving Tips**
    -
        - **Speed Limits**: On highways, the limit is 130 km/h (about 80 mph), while city driving is capped at 50 km/h (about 30 mph).
        - **Road Signs**: Italian road signs might be unfamiliar, so pay close attention. **Autovelox** (speed cameras) are common, and fines for speeding can be hefty.
        - **ZTL Zones**: Padua, like many Italian cities, has a **Zona a Traffico Limitato** (ZTL), which restricts access to the city center to local traffic only. Be careful not to drive into these zones, as fines are steep and sent directly to rental car companies.

4.   **Parking in Padua**
   -
      - **Park-and-Ride**: The **Piazzale Boschetti** and **Padova Ovest** parking lots offer affordable park-and-ride services into the city center. Both lots are linked to public transport, making it easy to leave your car and explore on foot or by tram.
      - **City Parking**: Paid parking lots, such as **Garage Roma** near Prato della Valle, charge around €1.50-2 per hour or €20-25 per day. Street parking is available but can be limited and expensive in the city center.

Insider Tip: If you're driving, consider staying at a hotel outside the ZTL zone with parking included and use public transport to get around.

Public Transport Options in Padua

Padua's public transport system is efficient and easy to navigate, with buses and trams connecting all major points of interest.

1.   **Tram System**

Padua's tram line runs from the northern suburbs to **Prato della Valle in** the south, passing through the city center and key attractions. Trams are frequent, clean, and an easy way to get around, especially for tourists staying near the main sites.

2.   **Bus System**

The city's extensive bus network complements the tram, offering connections to outlying neighborhoods and nearby towns. Buses run regularly, and most lines pass through **Piazza dei Signori** or the train station.

3.   **Ticket Options**
   -
      - **Single Tickets** Cost around €1.30 and are valid for 75 minutes on buses and trams.

- **Day Passes**: If you plan to take multiple trips, a 24-hour pass for €4.50 is a great deal.
- **Padova Card**: This tourist card offers free public transport for 48-72 hours, along with free or discounted entry to museums and attractions.

4.   **Where to Buy and How to Validate**

Tickets can be purchased at **tabacchi** shops, newsstands, and ticket machines at major stops. Don't forget to validate your ticket by stamping it in the machine on board—fines for unvalidated tickets can be steep!

5.   **Key Tourist Routes**
-
- Tram Line SIR1: Runs directly through the city's main attractions, including **Scrovegni Chapel** and **Prato della Valle**.
- Bus Line 3: Convenient for reaching the **Basilica of Saint Anthony** and **the University of Padua**.

Insider Tip: Download the **Muoversi Padova**app for real-time schedules and route maps, or visit the official **APS Mobilità** website.

Which Option Is Best for You?

Ultimately, your choice of transportation to Padua depends on your travel style. For international travelers, flying into Venice or Bologna is convenient and offers plenty of onward connections. Trains are ideal for exploring Italy's major cities and provide a stress-free option for day trips or longer stays. Driving allows for flexibility and scenic detours, but make sure to plan for parking and avoid the ZTL zones. Once in the city, Padua's tram and bus system make getting around a breeze, with affordable options for tourists.

Chapter 2: Top Attractions in Padua

Padua is a city that seamlessly blends its rich medieval heritage with a vibrant, modern vibe, offering visitors a treasure trove of history, art, and cultural experiences. Whether you're captivated by Giotto's breathtaking frescoes, the ancient halls of a world-renowned university, or the serene beauty of one of the world's oldest botanical gardens, Padua has something for everyone. Here's a look at the top attractions that should be on every visitor's list.

History and Cultural Significance

The **Scrovegni Chapel** is Padua's crown jewel of art history and
one of the most important monuments in Western art. Completed in
1305, this small chapel was commissioned by the wealthy Scrovegni
family as a private place of worship and a way to atone for their sins
(the family's wealth came from usury, a sin in medieval times). The
real star here is **Giotto di Bondone**, whose frescoes inside the
chapel mark a groundbreaking moment in art history. Giotto's work
paved the way for the Renaissance with his revolutionary use of
perspective, emotion, and naturalism.

Key Features

As soon as you step inside, you are enveloped by Giotto's
masterpiece. The walls are covered in a vivid sequence of frescoes
depicting the **Life of Christ and** the **Life of the Virgin**, along with
scenes from the **Last Judgment**. The expressive faces, delicate
details, and bold colors make it feel as if the events are unfolding
before your eyes. The stunning blue ceiling, dotted with golden
stars, adds to the chapel's heavenly atmosphere.

Practical Information

- **Opening Hours**: Daily from 9:00 AM to 7:00 PM
- **Tickets**: €14 per person (includes entrance to the Eremitani
  Museum)
- **Booking**: Tickets must be booked in advance, as only 25
  people are allowed inside every 15 minutes to protect the
  frescoes from humidity.
- **Tours**: Guided tours are available and highly recommended
  to get the most out of your visit.

Insider Tip

For the best experience, visit early in the morning or late afternoon to avoid the busiest times. Allow yourself to sit quietly and absorb the beauty—you'll feel like time has stopped. Make sure to visit the **Eremitani Museum afterward** to learn more about Padua's artistic heritage.

Nearby Attractions: After visiting the chapel, stroll through the nearby **Giardini dell'Arena** for a peaceful break in the gardens.

Basilica of Saint Anthony: A Pilgrim's Dream

History and Cultural Significance

The **Basilica of Saint Anthony**, known simply as "Il Santo" to locals, is one of the most revered pilgrimage sites in the world. This grand basilica was built to honor Saint Anthony, the beloved patron saint of lost things after he died in 1231. His tomb is housed here, and millions of visitors come each year to pay their respects, seeking miracles or solace.

Key Features

The basilica is an architectural marvel, blending **Romanesque, Gothic, and Byzantine** styles. Inside, you'll find the **Chapel of the Relics**, which holds Saint Anthony's tongue, jawbone, and vocal cords (yes, really!). The **Tomb of Saint Anthony** is the spiritual heart of the basilica, where visitors leave handwritten notes or touch the tomb in prayer. Don't miss **Donatello's bronze statues** of the high altar, which are masterpieces of Renaissance sculpture.

Practical Information

- **Opening Hours**: Daily from 6:20 AM to 7:45 PM
- **Tickets**: Free entrance, though donations are encouraged.

- **Tours**: Free guided tours are available, and they provide fascinating insights into both the religious and artistic significance of the basilica.

Insider Tip

Attend the daily Mass or just sit quietly and watch the faithful. Even if you're not religious, the atmosphere is deeply moving. Photography inside the basilica is restricted, so be respectful of the sacred space.

Nearby Attractions: After visiting the basilica, head over to the **Orto Botanico**, just a 10-minute walk away, for a peaceful retreat.

Prato della Valle: Europe's Largest Square

History and Cultural Significance

At nearly 90,000 square meters, **Prato della Valle** is the largest square in Italy and one of the largest in Europe. Originally a marshy area, it was transformed in the 18th century into the elegant public space it is today, complete with a central island surrounded by a canal and statues of 78 notable figures from Padua's past. Over the centuries, this square has been used for everything from jousting tournaments to public markets.

Key Features

The square's most distinctive feature is the **oval canal**, lined with statues of scholars, artists, and historical figures connected to the city. The surrounding **green spaces** are perfect for relaxing or having a picnic. On Saturdays, the square comes alive with **markets**, offering everything from fresh produce to antiques.

Practical Information

- **Opening Hours**: Open 24 hours
- **Tickets**: Free entry

- **Events**: Prato della Valle often hosts festivals, concerts, and cultural events throughout the year.

Insider Tip

If you visit on a Saturday, you can experience the local markets in full swing. It's a great place to pick up fresh fruit, local cheese, or handmade crafts. For a quieter experience, visit in the early morning or late afternoon when the light creates a magical atmosphere around the statues.

Nearby Attractions: Just steps away is the Basilica **of Saint Anthony**, making this an ideal combo visit.

Palazzo della Ragione: A Medieval Masterpiece

History and Cultural Significance

Built in the early 13th century, the **Palazzo della Ragione**was was once the seat of Padua's law courts and city council. Its **Salone**, the grand hall on the upper floor, is one of the largest medieval halls in Europe, and its walls are covered in hundreds of astrological frescoes. The hall's sheer size and intricate decoration reflect the power and wealth of medieval Padua.

Key Features

The **Salone is** the star of the show, with its enormous vaulted ceiling and walls covered in frescoes that depict the zodiac, planets, and various allegorical figures. One quirky feature is the **wooden horse**, a massive replica of a horse made for a medieval festival. Downstairs, you'll find **Piazza delle Erbe** and **Piazza della Frutta**, where vibrant daily markets take place.

Practical Information

- **Opening Hours**: Tuesday to Sunday, 9:00 AM to 6:00 PM
- **Tickets**: €6 for adults, €4 for students and seniors
- **Tours**: Audio guides are available, but for the full experience, opt for a guided tour to delve into the history of the frescoes and the building's legal past.

Insider Tip

Plan your visit to coincide with the daily markets in the piazza below the palazzo. After exploring the Salone, grab a coffee at one of the nearby cafes and watch the hustle and bustle of local life.

Nearby Attractions: The palazzo is located near the **University of Padua**, making it easy to visit both in one afternoon.

University of Padua: A Hub of Knowledge

History and Cultural Significance

Founded in 1222, the **University of Padua** is one of the oldest universities in the world and has been at the forefront of academic achievement for centuries. It is famously associated with **Galileo Galilei**, who taught here in the early 17th century. Today, the university remains a prestigious center of learning, particularly in the fields of medicine and science.

Key Features

A visit to the **Anatomy Theatre** is a must. This was the world's first permanent anatomical dissection theater, where medical students observed dissections to better understand human anatomy. You can also see **Galileo's podium**, where the famous scientist lectured. The **Palazzo Bo**, the main university building, is steeped in history, with its ancient courtyards and beautiful frescoes.

Practical Information

- **Opening Hours**: Guided tours run Monday to Saturday
- **Tickets**: €7 for a guided tour of Palazzo Bo, including the Anatomy Theatre
- **Tours**: Booking in advance is recommended, especially during peak tourist seasons.

Insider Tip

If you're interested in the history of science, don't miss the **Museo di Storia della Medicina**, which showcases the university's groundbreaking work in medical research.

Nearby Attractions: Just around the corner is **Caffè Pedrocchi**, one of Italy's oldest cafes and a perfect spot for an espresso after your visit.

Orto Botanico: A Green Oasis

History and Cultural Significance

The **Orto Botanico** is the oldest university botanical garden in the world, founded in 1545. Originally established to study medicinal plants, it's now a **UNESCO World Heritage Site** and a haven for plant lovers. The garden has been a center of scientific study for centuries, and many famous botanists have conducted research here.

Key Features

The garden is home to thousands of plant species, including rare and endangered plants. The **Goethe Palm**, planted in 1585, is one of its most famous residents—legend has it that this very tree inspired the poet Johann Wolfgang von Goethe during his travels. The modern **biodiversity garden showcases** plants from all over the world in climate-controlled glasshouses.

Practical Information

- **Opening Hours**: Daily from 9:00 AM to 7:00 PM (hours may vary seasonally)
- **Tickets**: €10 for adults, €8 for students and seniors
- **Tours**: Self-guided tours are available, but guided tours offer more insight into the history and scientific importance of the garden.

Insider Tip

The best time to visit is in late spring or early summer when the gardens are in full bloom. However, the **Biodiversity Garden** offers an interesting experience year-round.

Nearby Attractions: The **Basilica of Saint Anthony is** just a short walk away, making this a peaceful stop after exploring the city's religious heritage.

From the awe-inspiring frescoes of the **Scrovegni Chapel** to the serene beauty of the **Orto Botanico**, Padua's top attractions offer a unique blend of history, art, science, and culture. Whether you're a lover of Renaissance art, a history buff, or just someone looking for a beautiful place to wander, Padua has something special to offer. These sites not only tell the story of the city's past but also invite you to experience the vibrant life that still thrives here today.

Padua is not just a city of history and science but also a treasure trove of art and culture. From the ancient relics of Roman times to the visionary techniques that laid the foundation for modern cinema, Padua's museums offer a deep dive into the city's multifaceted artistic legacy. Whether you're an archaeology buff, a Renaissance art lover, or a film enthusiast, the city's museums are sure to fascinate.

Let's explore three of Padua's must-visit art institutions: The **Museo Civico agli Eremitani**, the **Museo del Precinema**, and the dynamic **temporary exhibitions scattered** throughout the city.

Museo Civico agli Eremitani: Archaeology and Renaissance Art

Overview and Significance

The **Museo Civico agli Eremitani** is one of Padua's most prestigious institutions, offering a journey through time with its dual focus on **archaeology and Renaissance art**. Located in a former monastery next to the Scrovegni Chapel, the museum houses an impressive collection of Roman artifacts, medieval frescoes, and Renaissance masterpieces. It's a must-see for visitors looking to understand the historical depth of Padua, from its ancient roots to its artistic golden age.

Key Collections

The museum's **archaeology section transports** visitors back to Padua's Roman past, showcasing mosaics, sculptures, and everyday objects that illustrate life in the ancient city. Among the highlights are the **Sarcophagus of Claudia Toreuma**, a beautifully carved Roman tomb, and the **mosaics from the Roman baths**, which provide a glimpse into the luxury of the era.

Moving into the **art gallery**, visitors will find works from the Middle Ages to the Renaissance, with a particular focus on artists from the Veneto region. Look out for the striking **Polyptych of Saint Luke** by **Giusto de' Menabuoi**, whose detailed depiction of saints and biblical scenes is a masterpiece of 14th-century Italian art. The museum's Renaissance collection includes works by Jacopo **Bellini** and **Giovanni Battista Piazzetta**, offering a visual feast of color, composition, and emotion.

Practical Information

- **Location**: Piazza Eremitani, Padua
- **Opening Hours**: Tuesday to Sunday, 9:00 AM – 7:00 PM
- **Tickets**: €10 (includes entrance to the Scrovegni Chapel)
- **Guided Tours**: Available on request, but make sure to book in advance to secure a spot.

Insider Tips

- **Combine Your Visit**: Since the museum is right next to the **Scrovegni Chapel**, it's easy to combine both in one visit.

Start with the museum to gain a deeper understanding of the period before immersing yourself in Giotto's frescoes.

- **Best Time to Visit**: Mornings are usually quieter, especially during weekdays. Avoid the early afternoon rush when group tours tend to visit.
- **Suggested Route**: If you're short on time, start with the Renaissance art collection on the upper floors and then move down to the archaeological section. Don't miss the Roman mosaics—they're stunning and often overlooked.

Compelling Reason to Visit: Where else can you experience the grandeur of ancient Rome, the beauty of Renaissance art, and the proximity of Giotto's groundbreaking frescoes, all under one roof?

Museo del Precinema: A Window into the Birth of Film
Overview and Significance

For film buffs, tech enthusiasts, or curious visitors of all ages, the **Museo del Precinema** offers a unique and engaging look at the world before cinema. Tucked away in **Palazzo Angeli**, this quirky little museum is dedicated to the optical devices that paved the way for moving pictures. From **magic lanterns** to **zoetropes**, the museum showcases how light, lenses, and imagination came together to create the magic of precinema. It's a delightful, interactive experience that connects the dots between centuries-old inventions and the blockbuster films of today.

Key Exhibits

The heart of the museum's collection is its **magic lanterns**, early image projectors that used painted slides to entertain audiences in the 18th and 19th centuries. These lanterns are incredibly detailed, with some slides offering animated scenes by having multiple layers move in front of light sources. Don't miss the collection of

zoetropes, devices that create the illusion of motion through rotating images—think of them as the first animated films!

In addition to the fascinating devices, the museum also delves into the historical context of precinema entertainment, showing how these innovations delighted audiences long before the age of cinema. It's not just about the machines but about how they sparked wonder and anticipation in people who had never seen moving images before.

Practical Information

- **Location**: Prato della Valle, Palazzo Angeli
- **Opening Hours**: Monday to Friday, 10:00 AM – 6:00 PM
- **Tickets**: €5 for adults, €3 for students and children
- **Interactive Exhibits**: Hands-on displays allow visitors to experiment with optical illusions and early animation techniques.

Insider Tips

- **Great for Families**: This museum is particularly engaging for families with children. The interactive exhibits make it a fun and educational experience for kids, offering a break from more traditional art galleries.
- **Special Demonstrations**: Check the museum's schedule for live demonstrations of how these devices worked—it's a treat to see a magic lantern show in action!
- **Nearby Attractions**: After your visit, take a leisurely walk around **Prato della Valle**, one of Europe's largest squares, and soak in the atmosphere.

Compelling Reason to Visit: Dive into the quirky and inventive world of precinema, where you'll discover the magical optical devices that brought stories to life long before the silver screen existed.

Temporary Exhibitions: Contemporary Art in Padua

Overview and Significance

While Padua is rich in historical art, the city also has a thriving contemporary art scene, with numerous venues hosting temporary exhibitions that showcase cutting-edge work from both Italian and international artists. These exhibitions offer an exciting contrast to the city's classical art and give visitors a glimpse into the modern cultural pulse of Padua.

Key Venues

- **Centro Culturale Altinate/San Gaetano**: This modern cultural center, housed in a former church, is one of the main venues for contemporary art exhibitions in Padua. The exhibitions here range from photography to sculpture and installations, often reflecting current social and political themes.
- **Palazzo Zabarella**: Known for its elegant architecture, this palazzo hosts rotating exhibitions that often focus on modern interpretations of classical themes or the works of 20th-century Italian artists.
- **Spazio Cartabianca**: This gallery is dedicated to emerging contemporary artists, offering a platform for experimental and avant-garde work in various mediums.

Annual Events

One of the highlights of Padua's contemporary art scene is the **Biennale del Disegno**, a biennial event that celebrates the art of drawing. It features exhibitions across multiple venues in the city and attracts both established and up-and-coming artists. Another key event is the **Padova Art Fair**, where collectors and art lovers gather to discover new works by contemporary artists.

Practical Information

- **How to Find Exhibitions**: Many of these temporary exhibitions are promoted on the websites of the venues or through the **Padova Cultura** portal, which provides up-to-date information on what's happening in the city's art scene.
- **Tickets**: Prices vary depending on the exhibition, but entry fees typically range from €5 to €12.

Insider Tips

- **Stay Updated**: If you're passionate about contemporary art, sign up for newsletters or check local cultural websites to keep track of what's on during your visit.
- **Best Time to Visit**: Temporary exhibitions can get crowded, especially during opening nights or weekends. For a quieter experience, visit during weekday mornings or early afternoons.

Compelling Reason to Visit: Padua's temporary exhibitions offer an ever-changing window into contemporary art, providing a fresh and dynamic perspective alongside the city's more historic treasures.

Padua's art and museum scene is as diverse as it is rich, offering something for every type of cultural traveler. From the ancient artifacts and Renaissance masterpieces at the **Museo Civico agli Eremitani** to the quirky and engaging world of **pre-cinema at Museo del Precinema** and the dynamic contemporary exhibitions across the city, Padua's artistic offerings span centuries of creativity. These museums not only celebrate the city's past but also keep its cultural scene alive and vibrant today. So whether you're an art lover or simply curious, Padua's museums will leave you inspired, enlightened, and ready to explore more.

Chapter 4: Exploring Padua's Religious Heritage

Padua, a city steeped in history, is also a place of profound spiritual significance. Known for its deep-rooted religious traditions and home to some of Italy's most important pilgrimage sites, Padua draws visitors from around the world seeking both spiritual reflection and an appreciation of its rich religious art and architecture. Whether you are:

- A pilgrim or a curious traveler.
- Exploring Padua's religious heritage will offer insights into its cultural soul.
- An opportunity to experience the city's living traditions.

Let's delve into the key religious sites, festivals, and traditions that make Padua a significant spiritual destination.

Overview of Padua as a Pilgrimage Destination

For centuries, **Padua** has been a vital destination for religious pilgrims, most famously associated with **Saint Anthony**, the beloved Franciscan saint known for his powerful intercessions, particularly in finding lost items and helping those in need. The **Basilica of Saint Anthony** is the heart of this pilgrimage tradition, but Padua's spiritual landscape extends beyond its most famous basilica. Pilgrims from all over the world come to pay their respects, seek blessings, and walk the same paths that millions before them have trodden.

Major Pilgrimage Sites

- **Basilica of Saint Anthony**: The Basilica is one of the most visited pilgrimage sites in the Christian world. Its connection to Saint Anthony, whose tomb lies within, draws the faithful seeking spiritual solace and miraculous intervention.

- **Santa Giustina Basilica**: Another important pilgrimage site, this church is dedicated to **Saint Justina**, a martyr who is venerated as one of the city's protectors. The church houses her relics and those of **Saint Luke the Evangelist**, making it a sacred space for pilgrims and art lovers alike.
- **Sanctuary of Arcella**: Located just outside the city, this sanctuary marks the place where **Saint Anthony** died. It's a quieter, less-touristed site but carries immense spiritual weight for devotees of the saint.

Spiritual Journey Through the City

Many pilgrims choose to take a **spiritual walk** through Padua, beginning at the Basilica of Saint Anthony, moving to **Santa Giustina**, and then out to the **Sanctuary of Arcella**. This journey offers a chance for reflection, prayer, and an intimate connection with the city's religious history. Along the way, pilgrims can stop at smaller chapels and lesser-known churches, many of which have their own unique stories and relics.

Lesser-Known Religious Sites

For those seeking a more off-the-beaten-path experience, the **Church of San Nicolò** offers a peaceful retreat away from the crowds. Built in the 11th century, this church is one of the oldest in Padua and provides a quiet space for contemplation.

Insider Tip: Start your pilgrimage early in the morning to avoid the heat and crowds. Along the way, you'll find many small cafes where you can stop for a reflective break with a cup of coffee.

Why It's a Hidden Gem

Tucked beside the grand **Basilica of Saint Anthony**, the **Oratory of San Giorgio** is one of Padua's lesser-known treasures. Often overlooked by tourists, this oratory is a true gem for those interested in religious art. Built-in the 14th century as a private chapel for the Lupi family, it boasts an extraordinary cycle of frescoes that rival some of the city's better-known masterpieces.

Key Features

The **fresco cycle** inside the oratory was painted by **Altichiero da Zevio**, a contemporary of Giotto, and depicts scenes from the lives of **Saint George, Saint Catherine**, and **Saint Lucy**. The frescoes are noted for their vibrant color, intricate details, and expressive figures. One standout is the depiction of **Saint George slaying the dragon**, a scene filled with dynamic movement and emotion.

Artistic Style and Comparisons

While often compared to Giotto's frescoes in the **Scrovegni Chapel**, Altichiero's work in the Oratory of San Giorgio is more intimate and personal, focusing on the lives of saints rather than grand biblical scenes. The oratory's small size allows visitors to get close to the artwork, providing an immersive experience.

Practical Information

- **Location**: Piazza del Santo, next to the Basilica of Saint Anthony
- **Opening Hours**: 9:00 AM – 1:00 PM, 2:00 PM – 6:00 PM (hours may vary)
- **Tickets**: €3 for adults, often included in combination tickets with the **Basilica of Saint Anthony** or **Scrovegni Chapel**

- **Access**: The oratory is often quieter than the nearby basilica, making it a peaceful place to reflect and enjoy the artwork in solitude.

Insider Tip**: If you're visiting the Basilica of Saint Anthony, take a few minutes to step inside the Oratory of San Giorgio. You'll often find it blissfully uncrowded, allowing you to appreciate the art in a serene setting.

Local Religious Festivals: The Saint Anthony Festival

Significance of the Saint Anthony Festival

The **Saint Anthony Festival** is the highlight of Padua's religious calendar, celebrated every year on **June 13th**, the anniversary of the saint's death. This festival is both a **spiritual pilgrimage** and a community celebration, attracting thousands of devotees from across Italy and around the world. For the people of Padua, Saint Anthony is not just a religious figure but a beloved protector, and the festival reflects the deep connection between the saint and the city.

Key Events of the Festival

- **Processions**: The main event of the festival is the **Procession of Saint Anthony**, where a relic of the saint is carried through the streets of Padua. The procession winds its way through the city, accompanied by prayers, hymns, and the sound of church bells.
- **Masses**: Throughout the festival, multiple **Masses** are held at the **Basilica of Saint Anthony**, including a solemn High Mass attended by religious leaders and local dignitaries.
- **Blessings**: One of the festival's most touching moments is the **Blessing of the Lilies**, where lilies, the flower associated with Saint Anthony, are blessed and distributed to pilgrims as symbols of peace and purity.

Other Notable Religious Festivals

- **Santa Giustina's Feast**: Held every **October 7th** at the **Basilica of Santa Giustina**, this festival honors Padua's other patron saint with processions and celebrations.
- **Christmas in Padua**: During December, the city's churches host a series of **Nativity scenes** and special Masses, making it a wonderful time to experience Padua's spiritual warmth.

Practical Information

- **Date**: June 13th (Saint Anthony Festival), October 7th (Santa Giustina's Feast)
- **Duration**: One day of major events, but celebrations and Masses take place throughout the week
- **What to Expect**: The city is packed during the Saint Anthony Festival, so plan ahead. Expect crowds, especially around the basilica, but also a joyous and welcoming atmosphere.

Insider Tip**: If you want to fully immerse yourself in the festival, arrive a day or two early to attend some of the preparatory Masses and avoid the heaviest crowds.

Sacred Etiquette: Tips for Visiting Religious Sites

General Rules for Respectful Behavior

When visiting religious sites in Padua—or anywhere in Italy—respect and reverence are key. Many of these spaces are active places of worship, and it's important to be mindful of those who are there to pray.

- **Dress Code**: Modesty is important when entering churches and religious buildings. Both men and women should cover their shoulders and knees. Scarves or shawls are handy for covering up if needed.

- **Silence**: Keep conversations to a minimum, especially near the altar or during services. Silence is often requested inside chapels and basilicas, and it's always respectful to comply.
- **Photography**: Always check if photography is allowed. In many cases, photography is forbidden inside churches to preserve the sanctity of the space or protect delicate artworks. When photography is permitted, avoid using flash.

Avoiding Disruption During Services

If you're visiting a site during **Mass** or other religious ceremonies, it's best to either participate quietly or wait until the service has ended to explore. Many visitors find attending a service adds to their experience, even if they don't fully understand the liturgy.

Participating in Religious Ceremonies

Visitors of all faiths are welcome to observe or participate in religious ceremonies, provided they do so respectfully. If you wish to attend Mass or other services, consider sitting toward the back and observing the behavior of locals to guide your own.

Insider Tip**: Bring a light scarf with you when visiting religious sites—it's a versatile accessory that can serve as a respectful covering for your shoulders or head, should it be required.

Exploring Padua's religious heritage offers visitors a deeper understanding of the city's cultural and spiritual heart. From the grand **Basilica of Saint Anthony** to the hidden beauty of the **Oratory of San Giorgio**, Padua's sacred spaces provide not only a connection to its past but also an opportunity for personal reflection. Whether you're a pilgrim seeking to walk in the footsteps of Saint Anthony or a traveler captivated by religious art, Padua's religious sites and festivals offer an enriching experience that touches both the soul and the senses.

Note: Always verify current access information, opening hours, and any restrictions for religious sites and events before planning your visit, as these may change over time.

Chapter 5: Dining in Padua: A Feast for the Senses

Padua is a city that knows how to eat. Nestled in the heart of the Veneto region, its cuisine is a reflection of its rich history, blending local traditions with seasonal ingredients to create a unique culinary experience. Whether you're sitting down to a plate of risotto in a cozy trattoria or wandering through the bustling local markets in search of fresh ingredients, Padua's food scene is sure to leave you satisfied—and craving more. Let's dive into the must-try dishes, best restaurants, Veneto's finest wines, and local food markets that make Padua a food lover's paradise.

Must-Try Dishes and Local Specialties

Paduan Cuisine: Where Tradition Meets Flavor

Paduan cuisine is deeply rooted in the bounty of its surrounding farmland, rivers, and mountains. While Italian food is world-famous, each region has its distinct flavors, and Padua is no exception. From hearty pasta to creamy risottos, the dishes here are a celebration of simplicity, freshness, and tradition. But don't be fooled—simple doesn't mean boring. Paduan chefs know how to elevate even the humblest ingredients into something extraordinary.

Risotto alla Padovana: A Creamy Delight

At the heart of Paduan cuisine is **Risotto alla Padovana**, a creamy risotto made with peas, onions, and sometimes bits of local pork or chicken. What sets this risotto apart is its velvety texture, achieved by stirring Arborio rice slowly with broth until it reaches the perfect consistency. The sweetness of the peas balances the richness of the meat, creating a dish that's both comforting and indulgent. Traditionally eaten in spring when fresh peas are in season, it's a quintessential Paduan dish.

- **Where to Try It**: Head to **Antica Trattoria dei Paccagnella**, a charming trattoria tucked away from the tourist crowds. Their risotto is made with peas harvested from nearby farms, ensuring a fresh, seasonal taste.
- **Insider Tip**: Risotto is best enjoyed with a glass of local **Prosecco** to cut through the creaminess.

Bigoli in Salsa: The Heart of Veneto

For pasta lovers, **Bigoli in Salsa** is a must-try. **Bigoli**is a thick, spaghetti-like pasta that's often made with whole wheat, giving it a hearty, rustic flavor. In the traditional **salsa**, you'll find a simple but flavorful mix of onions and anchovies, sautéed slowly to create a rich, umami-packed sauce. The anchovies melt into the onions, offering a salty, briny taste that perfectly complements the pasta's robust texture. This dish is often associated with **Good Friday**, as it's traditionally meatless, but it can be found year-round in Padua's best restaurants.

- **Where to Try It**: For an authentic experience, visit **Osteria dal Capo**, a cozy eatery near the **Piazza dei Signori**. Their Bigoli in Salsa is a local favorite, served with a generous sprinkle of fresh parsley.
- **Insider Tip**: Ask for a side of **radicchio**—the local bitter green adds a refreshing crunch to balance the richness of the dish.

Other Local Specialties

- **Prosciutto Veneto**: This air-dried ham from the Euganean Hills is milder than its Parma counterpart, with a slightly sweet, nutty flavor. It's often served with local bread and cheese.

- **Baccalà Mantecato**: A creamy dish made from whipped salt cod, garlic, and olive oil. It's traditionally spread on toasted bread or polenta for a satisfying snack.
- **Frittelle di Zucca**: For vegetarians, these fried pumpkin fritters, flavored with cinnamon and sugar, are a delicious seasonal treat, especially in the fall.

Compelling Reason to Visit: Whether it's the creamy richness of Risotto alla Padovana or the bold flavors of Bigoli in Salsa, Padua's local dishes are a testament to the city's love of simple, high-quality ingredients.

Best Restaurants, Trattorias, and Osterias

Understanding the Dining Scene

In Padua, there's a restaurant for every occasion, but it's important to know the difference between **restaurants**, **trattorias**, and **osterias**.

- **Restaurants**: More formal, often with a focus on multi-course meals and an extensive wine list.
- **Trattorias**: Informal, family-run establishments that serve traditional home-style cooking.
- **Osterias**: Casual, often serving simple dishes and local wines, perfect for a quick meal or a leisurely lunch.

Antica Trattoria dei Paccagnella

- **Signature Dish**: Risotto alla Padovana
- **Ambiance**: Warm and rustic, with wooden beams and checkered tablecloths.
- **Price Range**: €20-35 per person

- **Best Time to Visit**: Lunch is the perfect time to soak in the ambiance of this historic trattoria, but be sure to make a reservation as it fills up quickly.
- **Insider Tip**: Their house-made **tiramisu** is not to be missed—creamy, rich, and not too sweet.

Osteria dal Capo

- **Signature Dish**: Bigoli in Salsa
- **Ambiance**: Cozy and intimate, with just a handful of tables and walls adorned with vintage photos of Padua.
- **Price Range**: €15-25 per person
- **Best Time to Visit**: The evening is when locals come to unwind with a glass of wine and a plate of pasta.
- **Insider Tip**: Pair your Bigoli with a local glass of **Soave**, a crisp white wine that complements the anchovy sauce perfectly.

Le Calandre

- **Signature Dish**: Innovative takes on traditional Paduan dishes.
- **Ambiance**: A Michelin-starred restaurant that offers a modern, artistic approach to Veneto cuisine.
- **Price Range**: €150+ per person (tasting menu)
- **Best Time to Visit**: For a special occasion or an unforgettable culinary experience.
- **Insider Tip**: Book well in advance—this is one of Italy's top dining destinations.

Wine and Dine: Veneto's Best Wines

Veneto: A Wine Lover's Paradise

The **Veneto region** is one of Italy's most famous wine-producing areas, and Padua sits right at the heart of it. The rolling hills around the city are home to vineyards producing some of the country's best wines, from light and bubbly **Prosecco** to bold and complex

Amarone. Wine is a big part of the dining experience in Padua, and no meal is complete without a perfectly paired bottle.

Prosecco: The Sparkling Star

Prosecco is a light, bubbly wine that hails from the nearby Valdobbiadene region. Made primarily from **Glera grapes**, Prosecco is known for its fresh, fruity flavors and lively bubbles. It's the perfect wine for toasting a meal, and it pairs beautifully with many of Padua's dishes, especially light appetizers and fish.
- **Best Food Pairings**: **Baccalà Mantecato**, **Risotto alla Padovana**, or fresh seafood dishes.
- **Where to Taste**: For a real treat, visit **La Vecchia Enoteca**, a wine bar near **Piazza delle Erbe** that offers an excellent selection of local Proseccos. Their knowledgeable staff will guide you through a tasting experience.

Amarone: Rich and Velvety

On the other end of the spectrum is **Amarone**, a robust red wine from the **Valpolicella** region. Amarone is made using partially dried grapes, which concentrates the flavors and gives the wine its signature richness. With notes of cherry, chocolate, and spice, Amarone is the perfect wine for a hearty meal.
- **Best Food Pairings**: **Prosciutto Veneto**, rich pasta dishes, or aged cheeses.
- **Where to Taste**: Try **Enoteca dei Tadi**, a small but welcoming wine bar that specializes in Veneto's finest reds.

Other Notable Local Wines

- **Soave**: A crisp, dry white wine that pairs well with seafood and lighter pasta dishes.
- **Valpolicella Ripasso**: A more affordable cousin of Amarone, offering similar flavors but with a lighter body.

Compelling Reason to Visit: From light and effervescent Prosecco to the bold, velvety richness of Amarone, the Veneto region offers wine for every palate and occasion.

Chapter 6: Local Food Markets
The Soul of Padua's Culinary Scene

If you want to experience the heart of Paduan cuisine, there's no better place than the local markets. The **Piazza delle Erbe** and **Piazza dei Frutti** are the city's two main squares, and they've been home to bustling markets since medieval times. Today, these markets are where locals come to buy fresh produce, meats, cheeses, and all the ingredients that make Paduan cuisine so special.

Piazza delle Erbe: A Feast for the Senses

This market square is a vibrant hub of activity, with stalls selling everything from seasonal vegetables to fresh fish and local cheeses. The smell of ripe tomatoes and freshly baked bread fills the air, and the colorful displays of produce are enough to make any food lover's heart race.

- **Best Time to Visit**: Early morning is the best time to visit if you want to see the market in full swing.
- **What to Look For**: Don't miss the **Veneto asparagus** in the spring or the **wild mushrooms** in autumn. Local **cheeses** like **Asiago** are also a must-try.
- **Insider Tip**: Bring cash, as many vendors don't accept cards, and don't be afraid to chat with the sellers—they're always happy to offer cooking tips or tell you more about their products.

Piazza dei Frutti: Where Tradition Meets Modernity

Right next to **Piazza delle Erbe**, this market is known for its selection of meats, fish, and specialty products. The market's lively atmosphere makes it a great place to explore, even if you're just window shopping.

- **What to Look For**: Local **salumi**, fresh seafood, and artisanal products like olive oil and honey.
- **Insider Tip**: If you're visiting in autumn, try the **chestnuts**—roasted on open flames, they're a seasonal favorite.

Compelling Reason to Visit: The markets of Padua are a sensory experience, offering a glimpse into the city's culinary soul. Whether you're buying ingredients for a picnic or just soaking in the atmosphere, the markets are a must-visit for any food lover.

Dining in Padua is more than just a meal—it's an experience. From the creamy comfort of **Risotto alla Padovana** to the rich depths of **Amarone**, Padua's culinary scene reflects the city's history, traditions, and love of good food. Whether you're sipping wine at a cozy osteria, exploring the bustling markets, or savoring a plate of Bigoli in Salsa, each bite offers a taste of Padua's unique culinary identity.

Be adventurous in your culinary explorations, but also remember to respect local customs, especially in the markets and traditional eateries. Italians take their food seriously, and dining in Padua is a celebration of both flavor and culture.

Shopping in Padua: From Chic Boutiques to Artisan Treasures

Shopping in Padua is an adventure that takes you from the elegance of Italian fashion to the vibrant energy of its weekly markets, where local artisans display their handcrafted wares. This city offers a shopping experience that combines modern style with centuries-old craftsmanship, giving visitors a taste of both contemporary Italian trends and traditional artistry. Whether you're on the hunt for the latest designer clothing or a one-of-a-kind piece of pottery, Padua's shopping scene promises something special for every visitor. Let's dive into the best places to shop, from sleek boutiques to bustling markets.

Local Boutiques and Fashion Shopping
The Fashion Scene in Padua

Padua may not have the same fashion reputation as Milan or Florence, but don't let that fool you. This city is home to an array of **stylish boutiques that** cater to both high-end shoppers and those seeking more affordable chic. Padua's fashion scene reflects its place in the Veneto region, a historical hub of textile production and design. Here, you'll find a mix of **classic Italian elegance**, modern trends, and unique local designs, all within walking distance of the charming city center.

Key Shopping Streets and Areas

- **Via Roma**: One of Padua's main shopping streets, Via Roma is lined with a variety of **fashion boutiques** offering everything from luxury brands to trendy, affordable fashion. This is the place to start your shopping journey if you're looking for high-quality Italian clothing and accessories.
- **Galleria Borromeo**: For those who love designer labels, Galleria Borromeo offers a collection of high-end stores in a stylish, modern setting. Here, you can browse brands like **Armani**, **Prada**, and **Gucci** while sipping a cappuccino at one of the upscale cafes.
- **Via San Fermo**: For a more boutique shopping experience, Via San Fermo is where you'll find elegant shops catering to professionals and fashion-forward locals. This street is also home to several **fine jewelry** stores, perfect for those looking to take home a piece of Italian craftsmanship.

Must-Visit Boutiques

- **Michela R** (Via Roma 95): This chic boutique offers a curated selection of **Italian-made fashion** that blends timeless elegance with modern flair. Expect to find tailored dresses, high-quality coats, and stunning accessories that reflect the understated luxury Italy is known for.

- **Price Range**: Moderate to high-end
- **Target Audience**: Stylish professionals and fashion-conscious travelers
- **Blocco 31** (Via Umberto I): For younger shoppers or those looking for something trendy yet affordable, Blocco 31 is a must. This boutique offers a range of **trendy streetwear** and casual fashion that is perfect for exploring the city in style.
  - **Price Range**: Affordable to mid-range
  - **Target Audience**: Trendy youth and casual fashion lovers

Shopping Tips

- **Sales Seasons**: Twice a year, Italy's major cities, including Padua, have their **saldi** (sales) periods, usually in January and July. This is the perfect time to snag high-quality Italian fashion at a fraction of the price.
- **Shopping Etiquette**: Italians value personal service, so don't hesitate to ask for help or suggestions when shopping. A friendly **"Buongiorno"** (good morning) as you enter the store will go a long way!

Enticing Reason to Visit: Whether you're hunting for designer pieces or trendy streetwear, Padua's fashion boutiques offer the perfect blend of Italian sophistication and modern style, with something for every budget.

Artisan Souvenirs: Pottery, Ceramics, and Handcrafted Goods

A Tradition of Craftsmanship

Padua is a city that takes pride in its **artisanal traditions**, and no visit is complete without taking home a piece of its craftsmanship. For centuries, the surrounding region has been a center of **pottery and ceramics**, producing everything from everyday household items to intricate works of art. These handmade goods make for meaningful souvenirs, offering a connection to the region's rich cultural heritage.

Pottery and Ceramics

Padua's ceramics are known for their **vibrant colors** and **traditional motifs**, often inspired by the **Renaissance** and nature. Look for plates, bowls, and vases that feature intricate hand-painted designs, from floral patterns to geometric shapes, reflecting the Veneto region's historical influences.

- **Cittadella Ceramica** (Via Santa Lucia): This family-run workshop has been producing **handcrafted ceramics** for generations. Their pieces are known for their bold use of color and fine detailing, making each item a work of art in its own right.
  - **What to Buy**: Hand-painted plates, vases, and decorative tiles
  - **Price Range**: Mid-range to high-end, depending on the intricacy of the design

Other Handcrafted Goods

- **Glassware**: Though nearby Venice is the star of Italian glassmaking, Padua also offers beautiful **handblown glassware**, perfect for adding a touch of elegance to your home. Look for delicate wine glasses, colorful vases, and intricate ornaments.
- **Textiles**: For something softer, Padua's **artisan textile** shops offer handwoven linens, scarves, and tapestries that reflect the region's history of textile production.
- **Leather Goods**: Italian leather is renowned for its quality, and Padua's artisans craft everything from **handmade belts** and **wallets** to **custom shoes**.

How to Identify Authentic Artisanal Products

When shopping for artisanal goods, keep an eye out for **certificates of authenticity** or the **"Made in Italy"** label, which ensures that the product was crafted locally. Many shops will also allow you to see the artisans at work, providing a glimpse into the process behind these beautiful pieces.

Unique Souvenirs: If you want something truly special, consider buying a **custom-made ceramic** or glass piece that can be personalized to your taste—an unforgettable reminder of your time in Padua.

Enticing Reason to Visit: Handcrafted ceramics and artisanal goods from Padua are not just souvenirs; they're pieces of the city's history and culture made by skilled artisans who have perfected their craft over centuries.

Best Markets for Shopping: Weekly Markets at Piazza dei Signori

The Atmosphere of Piazza dei Signori

There's no better way to experience Padua's local life than by exploring its weekly markets. The **Piazza dei Signori**, a grand square in the heart of the city, hosts one of Padua's most vibrant markets. Every week, the piazza comes alive with vendors selling everything from fresh produce and local delicacies to vintage clothing and handmade crafts. The air is filled with the sounds of haggling, the aroma of freshly baked bread, and the laughter of locals catching up over their morning espresso.

What to Find at the Market

- **Fresh Produce**: The market is known for its colorful displays of **seasonal fruits and vegetables**, including local specialties like **Veneto asparagus** in the spring and **chestnuts** in the fall.
- **Local Cheeses and Meats**: Don't miss the chance to try **Prosciutto Veneto** or buy a wedge of **Asiago** cheese to enjoy later. Many vendors offer samples so you can taste them before you buy.

- **Handcrafted Goods**: The market is also a great place to find **handmade textiles**, **pottery**, and **leather goods**. These items are often more affordable than in the boutiques but still reflect the quality craftsmanship Padua is known for.

Practical Information

- **Market Days**: The market is held on **Tuesdays and Saturdays**, typically starting early in the morning and running until around 1:00 PM. Arrive early for the best selection and a chance to chat with the vendors.
- **Navigating the Market**: Take your time wandering through the stalls—this is the perfect place to practice your Italian and engage with the local culture. Bargaining isn't common in Italy, but vendors may offer a slight discount if you're buying multiple items.
- **Seasonal Specialties**: Depending on the time of year, you'll find different products on the market. In summer, look for **fresh figs** and **tomatoes**, while winter brings **hearty greens** and **dried fruits**.

Other Notable Markets

- **Piazza delle Erbe**: Another fantastic market square, **Piazza delle Erbe** is known for its **daily produce market**, offering the freshest fruits, vegetables, and local specialties. It's also a great place to pick up **herbs** and **spices**.
- **Prato della Valle Flea Market**: If you're in the mood for something vintage, the flea market at **Prato della Valle** (held on Sundays) is a treasure trove of **antique furniture**, **vintage clothing**, and **collectibles**.

Enticing Reason to Visit: Whether you're in search of fresh produce, artisan goods, or a lively atmosphere, the weekly markets in Padua offer a shopping experience that connects you with the local community and its traditions.

Shopping in Padua is a journey through Italian fashion, artisan craftsmanship, and vibrant market culture. From chic boutiques offering the latest trends to markets brimming with local flavor, this city provides a rich and varied shopping experience. Whether you're picking up a stylish outfit, a handcrafted ceramic, or a bundle of fresh produce from the market, every purchase in Padua carries with it a piece of the city's culture and history.

Final Note on Sustainable Shopping: When shopping in Padua, consider supporting **local artisans** and businesses that use sustainable practices. By choosing handmade products and locally sourced goods, you're not only taking home a unique piece of Padua but also contributing to the preservation of traditional craftsmanship and a greener, more responsible way of consuming. Happy shopping!

Chapter 7: Parks and Outdoor Spaces in Padua

Nature and History Intertwined

Padua is not just a city of art, culture, and history—it's also a haven for nature lovers. Whether you're drawn to grand, open squares, lush botanical gardens, or tranquil walks along historic canals, Padua offers a variety of outdoor experiences to suit every taste. The city's green spaces are more than just places to relax—they are steeped in history, culture, and natural beauty. Let's explore three of Padua's most inviting outdoor spaces: **Prato della Valle**, the **Orto Botanico**, and the walking and biking trails along the city's canals.

Prato della Valle: A Green Escape in the City

A Grand Square with a Serene Heart

Step into **Prato della Valle**, and you'll find yourself in one of Europe's largest public squares. This vast, elliptical space, covering nearly 90,000 square meters, feels like a world of its own—a peaceful green oasis in the midst of the bustling city. The square is an exquisite blend of nature and history, with a central island, **Isola Memmia**, encircled by a canal lined with 78 statues of prominent historical figures. Despite its grandeur, there's a welcoming, down-to-earth vibe that invites visitors to stroll, relax, and soak in the atmosphere.

Imagine walking along the canal, the gentle breeze carrying the scent of freshly cut grass, while locals jog by or gather for picnics on the island's grassy slopes. In the warmer months, you'll find families playing, students reading under the trees, and couples strolling hand in hand. It's a place where the rhythms of city life slow down, and nature takes center stage.

A Place for All Seasons

Prato della Valle is not just a park—it's a gathering place for the people of Padua. Throughout the year, it hosts various events, from weekend **flea markets** to summer **concerts and** seasonal festivals. On Saturdays, the square transforms into a lively market, with stalls selling everything from fresh produce to antiques. It's the perfect spot to grab a snack, browse local crafts, and people-watch as the square fills with energy.

In the spring and summer, the square is at its most vibrant, with flowers blooming around the canal and the island's trees providing welcome shade. Early mornings are ideal for a peaceful jog or yoga session, while late afternoons offer stunning golden light that's perfect for photography.

Historical Context and Transformation

Prato della Valle's current beauty is the result of centuries of transformation. In Roman times, this area was marshland, later becoming a venue for medieval fairs and even jousting tournaments.

It wasn't until the late 18th century that architect **Andrea Memmo** redesigned the square into the elegant space we see today. The statues that now line the canal were added during this period, representing scholars, artists, and statesmen who left their mark on Padua's history.

Practical Information

- **Location**: Southern end of the city center, easily accessible by foot or tram.
- **Opening Hours**: Open 24 hours.
- **Cost**: Free entry.
- **Best Time to Visit**: Early mornings for quiet strolls, late afternoons for the best light, and Saturdays for market days.

Insider Tip: Grab a gelato from one of the nearby cafes and find a spot on the grass—it's the perfect way to unwind and take in the beauty of this iconic square.

Compelling Reason to Visit: Whether you're picnicking on the island, browsing the weekend market, or simply enjoying a peaceful walk, Prato della Valle offers a relaxing and culturally rich escape right in the heart of the city.

Orto Botanico: Discovering Botanical Wonders

A Living Museum of Plants

The **Orto Botanico di Padova is** no ordinary garden—it's the world's oldest university botanical garden, a UNESCO World Heritage site, and a living museum of plant species from around the globe. Founded in **1545**, it was created for the study of medicinal plants, and today, it remains a place of learning, research, and conservation. Strolling through the Orto Botanico is like stepping into a green sanctuary, where centuries of scientific discovery and natural beauty come together.

Exploring the Garden's Layout

The garden is divided into distinct sections, each offering a different botanical experience. In the **Old Garden**, you'll find ancient medicinal plants growing in symmetrical, geometric beds, a nod to the garden's Renaissance origins. The centerpiece here is the famous **Goethe Palm**, planted in **1585 and** named after the German poet Johann Wolfgang von Goethe, who visited the garden and was inspired by its beauty.

Further along, the modern **Biodiversity Gardens showcase** plants from five different climates housed in sleek, glass-enclosed greenhouses. As you walk through, you'll encounter tropical ferns, cacti from arid deserts, and rare orchids, all thriving in their carefully controlled environments.

The Orto Botanico is not only a feast for the eyes, but also a delight for the senses—the scent of blooming jasmine in the summer, the rustle of bamboo leaves in the wind, and the vibrant colors of seasonal flowers make this garden a sensory experience.

Must-See Features

- **The Goethe Palm**: At over 400 years old, this ancient palm tree is one of the garden's most treasured residents. Its towering height and graceful fronds are a sight to behold, and it stands as a symbol of the garden's long history.
- **The Water Garden**: A tranquil spot featuring water lilies, lotus flowers, and aquatic plants, perfect for a quiet moment of reflection.
- **The Biodiversity Garden**: This section is a must-visit for anyone interested in plant conservation and global ecosystems. It's a fascinating look at how different plants adapt to their environments.

Practical Information

- **Location**: Near the Basilica of Saint Anthony.
- **Opening Hours**: Open daily, but hours vary by season (typically 9:00 AM – 7:00 PM in summer, 9:00 AM – 5:00 PM in winter).
- **Entrance Fee**: €10 for adults, discounts for students and seniors.
- **Guided Tours**: Available and highly recommended for those interested in the garden's history and scientific contributions.

Insider Tip: Visit in the late spring or early summer to see the garden in full bloom. For photographers, the early morning offers the best light and fewer crowds.

Compelling Reason to Visit: A visit to the Orto Botanico is both a peaceful retreat and a journey through the history of botanical science, offering a unique glimpse into the natural world's wonders.

Walking and Biking Trails Along Padua's Canals

A Journey Along the Waterways

Padua's network of **canals** is a reminder of its medieval past when these waterways were used for trade and transportation. Today, they offer a scenic backdrop for some of the city's most enjoyable outdoor activities. Whether you prefer a leisurely walk or a more invigorating bike ride, the trails along Padua's canals provide a peaceful escape from the busy city streets.

Exploring the Canal Trails

One of the best ways to experience Padua's canals is by following the **Piovego Canal**, which connects the city to the nearby **Brenta River**. This route takes you through some of the city's most picturesque areas, with tree-lined paths, charming bridges, and glimpses of historic buildings reflected in the water.

For a shorter, more urban route, the **Naviglio Interno**runs through the city center, offering a pleasant walk or bike ride past old stone bridges and waterside cafes. Along the way, you'll see locals walking their dogs, cyclists commuting, and artists sketching the scenery.

Points of Interest Along the Trails

- **Porta Ognissanti**: One of Padua's ancient city gates, this structure marks the starting point of several canal routes and offers a glimpse into the city's fortified past.
- **Giardini dell'Arena**: This lovely park is located along the canal and makes for a great stop to relax or enjoy a picnic after a long walk or bike ride.

Practical Information

- **Bike Rentals**: Bikes can be rented from several locations in the city center, including **La Bicicletta Verde** near the **train station**. Rentals typically cost around **€10-15 per day**.
- **Difficulty Levels**: Most of the canal paths are flat and well-maintained, making them suitable for all fitness levels. Walking trails are easy, while cycling routes can range from beginner to moderate, depending on the distance.
- **Safety Tips**: Cyclists should be aware of pedestrians, especially on busier trails, and always follow local traffic regulations.

Suggested Itineraries

- **Short Walk**: Start at **Porta Ognissanti** and walk along the **Naviglio Interno** toward the **Giardini dell'Arena** for a peaceful morning stroll. This route is perfect for a relaxing walk, with plenty of benches along the way to stop and enjoy the view.
- **Full-Day Bike Trip**: For those looking to explore more of Padua's surroundings, follow the **Piovego Canal** out of the city toward the **Brenta River**. This longer route offers

stunning views of the countryside and can be combined with a riverside picnic.

Compelling Reason to Visit: Whether walking or cycling, the canal trails offer a unique way to experience the beauty of Padua, with tranquil waters and scenic views that make for an unforgettable outdoor adventure.

Padua's parks and outdoor spaces provide a perfect balance of nature, history, and recreation. From the expansive beauty of **Prato della Valle** to the botanical wonders of the **Orto Botanico** and the peaceful canal trails, these green spaces offer a refreshing escape from the city's busy streets. Whether you're looking for a quiet spot to relax, a scenic route for biking, or a historical garden to explore, Padua's outdoor spaces promise something for every nature lover.

When exploring Padua's green spaces, remember to respect the environment. Follow local guidelines, dispose of waste properly, and practice **Leave No Trace** principles to help preserve these beautiful areas for future generations. Enjoy the beauty of Padua, and leave it as you found it!

Chapter 8: Local Festivals and Events in Padua

A Celebration of Tradition, Taste, and Talent

Padua is a city that loves to celebrate, with a vibrant cultural calendar full of festivals and events that capture the essence of its rich heritage. Whether it's the solemn beauty of the **Saint Anthony Festival**, the mouth-watering indulgence of **food and wine festivals**, or the soul-stirring performances at **music and theatre events**, Padua offers something for every traveler who wants to experience the city at its liveliest. Let's take a journey through Padua's most exciting festivals and events, where history, culture, and community come together in colorful displays of joy and tradition.

Saint Anthony Festival: Religious Processions and Celebrations

The Heart of Padua's Spiritual Life

Padua and **Saint Anthony** are inseparable. Known as the patron saint of lost things and a protector of the poor, **Saint Anthony** holds a special place in the hearts of the Paduan people. Every year on **June 13th**, the city comes alive to honor him with the **Saint Anthony Festival**, one of the most important religious events in Italy. Pilgrims from around the world flock to Padua to pay homage, turning the city into a sea of faith and devotion.

A Day of Devotion and Community

The **Saint Anthony Festival** is a deeply moving experience steeped in tradition. The day begins with **Masses held** at the **Basilica of Saint Anthony**, where the faithful gather to pray and seek blessings. The atmosphere is reverent, with the basilica's grand architecture and the rich aroma of incense setting the scene for a profound spiritual experience. Many visitors leave handwritten prayers at the saint's tomb, hoping for his intercession in their lives.

The highlight of the day is the **Procession of Saint Anthony**, where a relic of the saint is carried through the streets of Padua. The procession winds its way through the city, passing historic landmarks and drawing both locals and tourists who line the streets to watch. Banners flutter, church bells ring, and the sound of hymns fills the air as the procession moves toward the **Prato della Valle**.

Timeline of Key Moments

- **Morning**: Solemn Masses are held at the Basilica, starting as early as 7:00 AM.
- **Midday**: The basilica courtyard fills with pilgrims offering flowers and prayers.
- **Afternoon**: The grand procession begins around 5:00 PM, with the relic of Saint Anthony carried through the city streets, followed by thousands of faithful.
- **Evening**: The procession ends at Prato della Valle, where blessings are given, and the celebration culminates in a festive but still deeply respectful atmosphere.

Practical Information

- **Date**: June 13th, annually.
- **Location**: Primarily around the **Basilica of Saint Anthony** and the **city center**, with the procession ending in **Prato della Valle**.
- **Best Vantage Points**: The steps of the **Basilica** offer a close-up view of the start of the procession, while **Piazza dei Signori** and **Prato della Valle** are great spots for watching it pass.
- **How to Participate**: Visitors are welcome to join the Masses or watch the procession. To show respect, wear modest clothing (cover shoulders and knees) and keep a respectful silence during religious services.

Insider Tip

Arrive early to the Basilica if you want to secure a spot inside for one of the Masses. If you're not religious, the procession is still a sight to behold, offering a window into Padua's deep cultural and spiritual traditions.

Compelling Reason to Visit: Whether you're a pilgrim or simply an observer, the **Saint Anthony Festival offers** a moving glimpse into the heart of Padua's religious devotion, set against the backdrop of the city's beautiful historic streets.

Food and Wine Festivals: The Best of Padua's Culinary Traditions

A Celebration of Taste and Tradition

In Padua, food is more than just sustenance—it's a celebration of life. The city's **food and wine festivals are** a chance for locals and visitors alike to come together and indulge in the culinary delights of the Veneto region. These festivals showcase the best of Paduan cuisine, from traditional dishes like **Risotto alla Padovana**to to the region's world-famous **Prosecco** and **Amarone wines**. They're also a chance to connect with local producers, chefs, and food lovers, all eager to share their passion for Padua's rich gastronomic heritage.

Notable Food and Wine Festivals

La Fiera delle Campanelle (The Bell Fair)

One of Padua's oldest festivals, **La Fiera delle Campanelle**, takes place in early **September in** the **Prato della Valle**. Originally a fair for selling ceramic bells, it has evolved into a celebration of local artisans and food producers. Stalls offer **regional specialties**, including artisanal cheeses, cured meats, and sweet treats like **frittelle di zucca**(pumpkin fritters). It's the perfect place to pick up unique souvenirs or enjoy a delicious street food meal.

- **What to Expect**: Food stalls, artisanal crafts, live music, and family-friendly activities.
- **Dates**: First weekend of September.
- **Location**: **Prato della Valle**.
- **Entry**: Free, with food available for purchase.

Padova Wine Festival

Held in **late spring**, the **Padova Wine Festival** is a must for any wine lover. The festival brings together vineyards from across the Veneto region to offer tastings of their finest wines, including **Prosecco**, **Soave**, **Amarone**, and **Valpolicella Ripasso**. Along with wine tastings, visitors can enjoy **cooking demonstrations**, pairing workshops, and meet-and-greets with local winemakers.

- **What to Expect**: Wine tastings, food pairings, and educational seminars on Veneto wines.
- **Dates**: May, annually.
- **Location**: Various venues across Padua, including **Piazza della Frutta** and **Palazzo della Ragione**.
- **Entry**: Entry to the festival is typically free, but tastings require purchasing a ticket (€10-20 for a tasting pass).

Tips for Navigating Food Festivals

- **Arrive Hungry**: With so much delicious food on offer, you'll want to sample as much as possible. Many festivals offer small portions, so you can try a variety of dishes.
- **Plan Ahead**: Popular events like the **Padova Wine Festival** can get crowded, especially on weekends, so consider attending on a weekday if you prefer a more relaxed atmosphere.
- **Don't Miss the Local Specialties**: Look out for dishes that are unique to the region, such as **Risotto alla Padovana** or **Bigoli in Salsa**.

Insider Tip

Bring cash! While most vendors accept cards, many smaller stalls at these festivals prefer cash for small purchases.

Compelling Reason to Visit: Padua's food and wine festivals are a feast for the senses, offering an authentic taste of the region's culinary traditions in a lively and communal atmosphere.

Music and Theatre Performances: Opera and Classical Concerts

A City of Artistic Excellence

Padua's cultural scene is as rich as its history, and music and theatre are at the heart of the city's artistic life. Whether it's the grand notes of **Italian opera** or the stirring strings of a **classical concert**, Padua's performance venues offer a diverse program that appeals to both locals and visitors alike. The city is home to some of Italy's most respected theatres and concert halls, as well as a calendar full of **open-air performances** that take advantage of the city's beautiful squares and parks.

Key Venues for Performances

Teatro Verdi

The **Teatro Verdi** is Padua's premier venue for opera and classical music, housed in a historic building that dates back to **1751**. The theatre's opulent interior, complete with gilded balconies and rich red velvet seating, offers the perfect backdrop for experiencing Italy's greatest art form—opera. Throughout the year, **Teatro Verdi** hosts a variety of performances, from full operas to intimate chamber music concerts.

- **What to Expect**: Performances of Italian classics, from **Puccini** to **Verdi**, along with contemporary works and international tours.
- **Location**: **Via dei Livello 32**, Padua.

- **Tickets**: Prices vary depending on the performance, ranging from €20 for concerts to €100+ for premium opera seats.

Palazzo Zuckermann Open-Air Concerts

In the warmer months, Padua's music scene spills out into the open, with **open-air concerts** held at various locations around the city. One of the most popular venues is the courtyard of **Palazzo Zuckermann**, where visitors can enjoy **classical music** under the stars. These concerts often feature emerging artists and offer a more informal, laid-back atmosphere.

- **What to Expect**: Classical concerts in a relaxed outdoor setting, with performances by local orchestras and international guest musicians.
- **Location**: **Corso Garibaldi**, Padua.
- **Tickets**: Typically free or low-cost (€10-20).

Annual Music and Theatre Events

Settimane Musicali al Teatro Olimpico

Every **spring**, Padua's cultural calendar kicks off with the **Settimane Musicali al Teatro Olimpico**, a prestigious festival that brings together some of the world's best classical musicians. While the festival's main events take place at the nearby **Teatro Olimpico** in **Vicenza**, Padua often hosts satellite performances featuring orchestras and soloists performing works by **Mozart**, **Beethoven**, and **Bach**.

- **Dates**: May to June.
- **Locations**: Various venues across Padua.
- **Tickets**: Prices vary, typically ranging from €30 to €80 for main events.

Insider Tip

For opera performances at **Teatro Verdi**, opt for the dress **circle** seats for the best views and acoustics. Also, remember that formal attire is appreciated, especially for evening performances.

Compelling Reason to Visit: Whether you're an opera enthusiast or just a fan of live music, Padua's music and theatre performances offer a cultural experience that combines world-class talent with the city's historic charm.

Padua's festivals and events offer visitors a chance to experience the city's soul, from the reverent processions of the **Saint Anthony Festival** to the lively flavors of **food and wine celebrations**, and the moving performances at its **theatres and concert halls**. Each event provides a unique window into the traditions, tastes, and artistic achievements that make Padua so special.

When attending Padua's festivals, be mindful of the local customs, especially during religious events like the **Saint Anthony Festival**. Show respect for the traditions, participate thoughtfully, and remember to support local businesses and artisans at food and wine festivals. This not only enriches your experience but also ensures that these cherished events continue to thrive for future generations.

Chapter 9: Nightlife and Entertainment in Padua

From Evening Hangouts to Live Performances

As the sun sets over Padua, the city transforms into a lively hub of activity where locals and visitors alike come together to enjoy the vibrant nightlife. With historic squares bustling with evening crowds, charming bars serving up signature cocktails, and intimate venues showcasing live music and theatre, Padua has a little something for every night owl. Whether you're seeking a quiet aperitivo with a view, an evening of live jazz, or a late-night café experience, Padua's nightlife offers plenty to explore. Let's dive into some of the best spots to experience the city's after-dark scene.

Evening Hangouts: Piazza delle Erbe and Piazza della Frutta

The Heartbeat of Padua's Nightlife

By day, **Piazza delle Erbe** and **Piazza della Frutta** are bustling markets where vendors sell fresh produce, local delicacies, and artisanal goods. But as the stalls pack up and the sun begins to dip below the horizon, these two iconic squares undergo a magical transformation. The markets give way to a vibrant evening scene, with bars and restaurants spilling out onto the cobblestone streets and locals gathering for drinks, dinner, and lively conversation.

The energy in these squares is infectious. By 7:00 PM, the tables lining the piazzas are filled with groups of friends, couples, and students enjoying an **aperitivo**, a beloved Italian tradition that's part pre-dinner drink, part social ritual. As you sip your **Spritz Aperol** or **Hugo**, the gentle hum of conversation fills the air, blending with the clinking of glasses and the occasional laughter from a nearby table. The glowing lights from the surrounding palazzi cast a warm glow over the scene, giving it an almost cinematic quality.

Popular Spots Around the Squares

- **Caffè dei Signori** (Piazza dei Signori): Overlooking **Piazza dei Signori**, this spot is ideal for an aperitivo. Enjoy a signature **Spritz** with a view of the **Torre dell'Orologio** (Clock Tower), watching the city shift from day to night.
- **Bar Nazionale** (Piazza delle Erbe): A local favorite, this bar offers a more casual vibe, with students and young professionals gathering for affordable drinks and light snacks like **cicchetti** (small Venetian-style tapas).
- **Caffè Pedrocchi** (Via VIII Febbraio): Just steps from Piazza delle Erbe, this historic café is perfect for a more sophisticated evening, offering fine wines and Paduan delicacies. Established in 1831, it's one of Italy's most famous literary cafés, and the elegant interior will transport you back in time.

Tips for Experiencing the Squares Like a Local

- **Aperitivo Time**: The aperitivo ritual usually kicks off around 6:00 PM and lasts until about 8:00 PM. Locals typically pair their drinks with small plates of snacks, so don't hesitate to order some light bites like **olives**, **prosciutto**, or **local cheeses**.
- **Best Time to Visit**: Arrive between 7:00 and 8:00 PM to snag a good spot. The squares are lively until around 11:00 PM when the bars start to close, and the crowd shifts to late-night cafés and pubs.
- **Local Customs**: Padua's aperitivo culture is all about socializing. Don't rush—enjoy your drink, chat with friends, and take in the atmosphere. It's not uncommon for locals to spend hours sipping slowly and people-watching.

Regular Events and Performances

Throughout the year, **Piazza delle Erbe** and **Piazza della Frutta** host a variety of **seasonal events**, from **Christmas markets** to **open-air concerts** in the summer. If you're lucky, you might catch a live performance or cultural event while enjoying your evening drink.

Insider Tip: For a quieter, more intimate experience, visit these squares on a weekday evening. Weekends tend to be bustling with both locals and tourists, but weekdays offer a more relaxed atmosphere.

Compelling Reason to Visit: With their lively evening scenes and historical surroundings, **Piazza delle Erbe and Piazza della Frutta** offers the perfect setting for an unforgettable night out in Padua— where every glass of wine and conversation seems to sparkle under the city's lights.

Best Bars and Cafes for a Night Out

The Bar Scene in Padua

Padua may be known for its history and art, but its **bar and café scene** is just as impressive. Whether you're looking for a sophisticated cocktail bar, a cozy wine bar, or a lively student hangout, the city has it all. From classic Italian aperitivi to trendy cocktails, Padua's bars offer a diverse range of experiences for a night out.

Recommended Bars and Cafes

Café Venezia

One of Padua's most iconic cafes, **Café Venezia**is, is located near **Piazza delle Erbe** and has been a fixture of the city's nightlife for years. By day, it's a quaint spot for coffee, but by night, it transforms into a stylish wine bar. The ambiance is refined yet welcoming, with soft jazz playing in the background and a polished interior that gives it a sophisticated charm.

- **Signature Drink**: **Negroni Sbagliato** (a twist on the classic Negroni, made with Prosecco instead of gin).
- **Price Range**: Mid-range (€8-12 for cocktails).
- **Best Time to Visit**: Early evening, around 8:00 PM, for a relaxing aperitif before heading to dinner.
- **Target Audience**: Professionals and couples looking for a refined yet relaxed evening.

La Yarda

A hipster haven located near the **University of Padua**, **La Yarda** is known for its creative cocktails and craft beers. The bar is a favorite among students and young professionals, offering a laid-back, artsy vibe with quirky décor and eclectic music playlists. The outdoor seating is particularly popular during the warmer months, making it a great spot for an open-air night out.

- **Signature Drink**: **Craft beers** and quirky cocktails like the **Lavender Gin Fizz**.
- **Price Range**: Affordable (€5-8 for drinks).
- **Best Time to Visit**: Late evening (9:00-11:00 PM), especially if you're looking for a lively, social atmosphere.
- **Target Audience**: Trendy, artsy crowd and students.

Enoteca da Severino

If you're a wine lover, **Enoteca da Severino** is the place to be. This charming wine bar near **Piazza dei Signori offers** a fantastic selection of Veneto wines, from crisp whites like **Soave**to to bold reds like **Amarone**. The ambiance is intimate and cozy, with dim lighting and rustic décor that makes it the perfect spot for a romantic evening or a quiet night with friends.

- **Signature Drink**: **Amarone** or **Prosecco**, paired with a cheese and charcuterie board.
- **Price Range**: Mid-range (€6-10 for a glass of wine).
- **Best Time to Visit**: 8:00-10:00 PM for a relaxing post-dinner drink.

- **Target Audience**: Wine enthusiasts and couples.

Bar Etiquette and Tipping Customs

- **Ordering Drinks**: Most bars in Padua don't offer table service in the evening, so you'll need to order at the bar. Don't forget to ask about **Cicchetti** or other snacks that might be available.
- **Tipping**: Tipping isn't expected in Italy, but it's always appreciated that you round up the bill or leave a euro or two for good service.

Compelling Reason to Visit: Whether you're in the mood for a quiet glass of wine or a lively cocktail, Padua's diverse bar scene offers a little something for everyone, from cozy enotecas to trendy hangouts.

Live Music Venues and Theatre Performances

A City Alive with Music and Performance

Padua's nightlife isn't just about bars and cafés—it's also a city that loves its **live music** and **theatre**. Whether you're in the mood for an intimate jazz performance or a grand classical concert, Padua offers a variety of venues to suit every taste. From historic theatres to modern music clubs, the city's evening entertainment scene is as diverse as it is exciting.

Live Music Venues

Q-Bar

One of Padua's top live music venues, **Q-Bar**is is known for its eclectic lineup of performances, ranging from **jazz and blues** to **indie and rock**. Located near **Prato della Valle**, it's a favorite among locals and visitors alike for its casual atmosphere and consistently great music.

- **Genre**: Jazz, blues, and indie rock.
- **Price Range**: Affordable (€10-15 for entry, depending on the event).
- **Best Time to Visit**: Check the schedule for performances, but most start around 9:00 PM.
- **Target Audience**: Music lovers of all ages.

Palazzo Zuckermann

For those who prefer classical music, **Palazzo Zuckermann** offers a more refined experience with regular **chamber music concerts** and recitals. The intimate setting of the palazzo provides an up-close and personal experience with some of Italy's best classical musicians, making it a must for any classical music fan.

- **Genre**: Classical music and chamber music.
- **Price Range**: Mid-range (€20-40 for concert tickets).
- **Best Time to Visit**: Performances typically begin at 8:00 PM.
- **Target Audience**: Classical music lovers and culture enthusiasts.

Theatre Performances

Teatro Verdi

The historic **Teatro Verdi** is the heart of Padua's theatre scene, offering everything from grand **opera performances** to **theatrical productions**. Built-in the 18th century, the theatre's opulent interior makes every performance feel like a special occasion. Throughout the year, the theatre hosts a diverse lineup of shows, including both Italian and international productions.

- **Genres**: Opera, theatre, and classical concerts.
- **Price Range**: Varies by performance (€20-100 for tickets).

- **Language Considerations**: While most performances are in Italian, you can often find translations or summaries available in the programs.
- **Best Time to Visit**: Performances typically begin at 7:30 PM or 8:00 PM.

Tips for Enjoying Live Performances

- **Dress Code**: For opera or theatre performances, semi-formal attire is appreciated, though smart casual is usually acceptable.
- **Booking Tickets**: It's best to book your tickets in advance, especially for popular performances at **Teatro Verdi** or **Palazzo Zuckermann**.

Compelling Reason to Visit: Padua's live music and theatre scene offers something for every taste, whether you're a fan of jazz, classical music, or a grand night at the opera.

Padua may be a city of history and academia by day, but by night, it transforms into a vibrant hub of nightlife and entertainment. Whether you're sipping cocktails in **Piazza delle Erbe**, enjoying live jazz at **Q-Bar**, or watching an opera at **Teatro Verdi**, the city's after-dark scene promises memorable experiences for every traveler.

Final Note on Responsible Nightlife: While Padua's nightlife is lively, remember to be respectful of the city's quieter residential areas, especially after midnight. Drink responsibly, if you must, and plan your journey home—whether it's by walking, public transport, or taxi—so you can enjoy your night out safely and responsibly.

Chapter 10: Day Trips from Padua
Discovering the Veneto Region

While Padua is brimming with history, culture, and charm, its location makes it the perfect base for exploring some of the Veneto region's most remarkable destinations. Whether you're seeking the enchantment of Venice, the natural beauty and medieval villages of the Euganean Hills, or the rich history of Vicenza and Verona, day trips from Padua offer a diverse range of experiences. In just a short train ride or scenic drive, you can find yourself wandering through iconic canals, sipping wine in a tranquil vineyard, or admiring ancient Roman amphitheaters. Let's dive into three unforgettable day trips from Padua.

Venice: The Perfect Day Trip

A City Like No Other

Venice, often referred to as **La Serenissima** (the Most Serene), is a city that seems to defy logic. Built on a network of canals, with its iconic gondolas, grand palaces, and centuries-old bridges, Venice is a destination that has captured the imaginations of travelers for generations. From Padua, Venice is just a short train ride away, making it an easy and enchanting day trip.

As you step out of **Santa Lucia Train Station**, the Grand Canal unfolds before you, an instantly breathtaking sight. Gondolas and vaporettos (water buses) glide along the water, and the sounds of Venice—lapping water, the call of gondoliers, and the gentle hum of life on the lagoon—draw you into the magic of this floating city.

Must-See Sights for a Day in Venice

To make the most of a day trip to Venice, a well-planned itinerary is essential. Here's a suggested route that hits all the highlights while leaving time for a few quieter, authentic Venetian moments.

·   **Morning: Piazza San Marco**

Start your day in the heart of Venice at **Piazza San Marco**, where the grandeur of **St. Mark's Basilica** and the towering **Campanile will** take your breath away. Step inside the basilica to admire the glittering mosaics, or, if you have time, climb the Campanile for panoramic views over the city and the lagoon.

·   **Mid-Morning: Bridge of Sighs and Doge's Palace**

Just around the corner from St. Mark's Basilica, you'll find the **Doge's Palace**, a Gothic masterpiece that was once the seat of Venetian power. After exploring the grand halls and crossing the famous **Bridge of Sighs**, pause to imagine the sighs of prisoners seeing their last view of Venice before being taken to the dungeons.

·   **Lunch: Venetian Cicchetti**

For lunch, avoid the tourist traps around Piazza San Marco and head to a **bacaro**(a traditional Venetian tavern) to enjoy **cicchetti** small plates of local specialties. Try **sarde in saor** (marinated sardines) or **baccalà mantecato** (creamed cod), paired with a glass of **Prosecco**.

·   **Afternoon: Rialto Bridge and the Grand Canal**

After lunch, stroll over to the famous **Rialto Bridge**, where you'll be treated to one of the best views of the Grand Canal. From there, take a **vaporetto** along the canal to see Venice's stunning palazzi and enjoy the city from the water.

·   **Late Afternoon: Cannaregio or Dorsoduro**

Escape the crowds and explore the quieter neighborhoods of **Cannaregio**or **Dorsoduro**. In Cannaregio, you can visit Venice's historic Jewish Ghetto, while Dorsoduro offers art lovers the **Gallerie dell'Accademia**, home to works by Venetian masters like **Tintoretto and Bellini**.

Practical Information

- **How to Get There**: Trains run frequently from **Padua to Venice Santa Lucia**, with the journey taking about **25-30 minutes**. A round-trip ticket costs around **€9-12**. Once in Venice, purchase a **Vaporetto pass** to navigate the canals.
- **Best Time to Visit**: Venice can be crowded year-round, but visiting in the early morning or late afternoon helps you avoid the midday rush. **Spring and fall** are ideal times for cooler weather and fewer crowds.
- **Cost**: Entry to St. Mark's Basilica is free, though the **Pala d'Oro** and **Doge's Palace** have entrance fees (around **€10-20**).

Insider Tips for Avoiding Crowds

- Visit **Piazza San Marco** either first thing in the morning or after 5:00 PM, when the day-trippers start to leave.

- Wander off the main tourist paths. Venice's true charm is found in its quieter neighborhoods, where locals still hang their laundry between canals and small, unassuming churches house hidden masterpieces.

Enticing Reason to Visit: Whether it's the shimmering canals, the architectural splendor, or the hidden alleyways waiting to be explored, Venice is a city that must be seen and believed. And from Padua, it's just a stone's throw away.

Exploring the Euganean Hills
{Wine, Nature, and Medieval Villages}

A Scenic Escape from the City

Just a short drive or bike ride from Padua, the **Euganean Hills**(Colli Euganei) offers a serene escape into nature, complete with rolling vineyards, thermal springs, and charming medieval villages. The hills, formed by ancient volcanic activity, rise unexpectedly from the Venetian plain, creating a dramatic landscape dotted with castles, monasteries, and lush greenery. It's the perfect destination for a day trip focused on **wine tasting**, **hiking**, and **exploring history**.

Highlights of the Euganean Hills

·   **Wine Tasting at Local Wineries**

The Euganean Hills are known for their excellent **wines**, particularly **Colli Euganei Fior d'Arancio**, a fragrant white wine made from **Moscato** grapes. Many wineries offer tours and tastings, allowing visitors to sample not only Fior d'Arancio but also **Merlot**, **Cabernet Sauvignon**, and local **sparkling wines**.

Cantina Vignalta: One of the most renowned wineries in the region, Vignalta offers tastings paired with local cheeses and charcuterie set against the backdrop of the scenic hills.

· **Medieval Charm in Arquà Petrarca**

One of the most beautiful villages in Italy, **Arquà Petrarca** is a step back in time. Named after the poet **Francesco Petrarca**, who spent his final years here, the village is a treasure trove of cobblestone streets, ancient stone houses, and panoramic views of the hills. Visit **Petrarca's House**, a museum dedicated to the poet, or simply wander the charming streets.

· **Nature and Hiking Trails**

The **Parco Regionale dei Colli Euganei** is a protected area that offers numerous **hiking** and **cycling trails** for outdoor enthusiasts. Trails wind through dense forests, past ancient monasteries, and up to hilltop castles. The **Monte Fasolo** loop is a popular trail offering stunning views of the surrounding countryside.

Practical Information

- **How to Get There**: The Euganean Hills are about **20-30 minutes by car** from Padua. If you prefer not to drive, consider joining a **guided wine tour** from Padua or renting a bike to explore the region.
- **Best Time to Visit**: Spring and fall are the best times to visit, as the weather is mild and the vineyards are either in bloom or harvesting.
- **Cost**: Wine tastings typically range from **€10-25**, depending on the winery and tasting package.

Insider Tips for Exploring the Hills

- **Wine Tasting Etiquette**: When visiting wineries, it's customary to book in advance. Most tastings include a tour of the vineyards and cellars, so allow time to learn about the winemaking process.

- **Scenic Routes**: If driving, take the **Strada del Vino dei Colli Euganei**, a scenic wine road that connects many of the region's top wineries and villages.

Enticing Reason to Visit: With its picturesque landscapes, rich history, and world-class wines, the Euganean Hills offers a perfect blend of relaxation and exploration—just a short journey from Padua.

Vicenza and Verona

(More History and Culture Beyond Padua)

Vicenza: The City of Palladio

Vicenza, a UNESCO World Heritage site, is often called the **City of Palladio** in honor of **Andrea Palladio**, one of the most influential architects of the Renaissance. His elegant, symmetrical villas and palaces can be seen throughout the city, giving Vicenza a refined and harmonious atmosphere. For architecture lovers, a day trip to Vicenza is a must, offering a chance to explore Palladio's masterpieces firsthand.

- **Key Attractions in Vicenza**:
  - **Teatro Olimpico**: Designed by Palladio, this indoor theatre is the oldest of its kind in the world, with an incredible stage set that gives the illusion of a long, open street.
  - **Villa La Rotonda**: Just outside the city, this iconic Palladian villa is known for its perfect symmetry and elegant design. It's often regarded as one of the most beautiful villas in Italy.

Verona: The City of Love and Roman Heritage

Verona, famously known as the setting for **Shakespeare's "Romeo and Juliet,"** is much more than a romantic destination. Its Roman history, magnificent architecture, and lively piazzas make it a dynamic city worth visiting. The heart of Verona's historical allure is its well-preserved Roman amphitheater, **Arena di Verona**, which still hosts **opera performances** during the summer months.

- **Key Attractions in Verona**:
  - **Arena di Verona**: Built in the 1st century AD, this Roman amphitheater is an incredible feat of engineering. In the summer, it becomes one of the world's most magical opera venues.
  - **Juliet's Balcony**: A pilgrimage site for lovers from around the world, **Casa di Giulietta** offers a glimpse into the legend of Romeo and Juliet.

Practical Information

- **How to Get There**: Both **Vicenza** and **Verona** are easily accessible by train from Padua. Vicenza is just **25 minutes away**, while Verona is about **45 minutes**. Round-trip tickets typically cost around **€9-15**.
- **Best Time to Visit**: Both cities can be visited year-round, but spring and early fall offer the best weather for exploring.
- **Cost**: Entrance fees for major attractions like the **Teatro Olimpico** and **Arena di Verona** range from **€6-15**.

Insider Tips for Vicenza and Verona

- **Vicenza**: Don't miss a stroll down **Corso Palladio**, the city's main street, lined with Palladian buildings and stylish shops.
- **Verona**: If you're visiting in summer, book tickets to an **opera at the Arena** well in advance, as performances often sell out.

Enticing Reason to Visit: From the architectural elegance of Vicenza to the romantic allure of Verona, these cities offer a perfect mix of history, culture, and unforgettable experiences, all within easy reach of Padua.

Each of these day trips offers a unique glimpse into the beauty and diversity of the Veneto region. Whether you're gliding down the canals of Venice, tasting wines in the Euganean Hills, or exploring the architectural wonders of Vicenza and Verona, you'll find that Padua is the perfect starting point for adventures beyond the city.

When visiting these destinations, be mindful of local customs, respect historical sites, and support small, local businesses. Travel thoughtfully, leaving behind only footprints and taking with you the memories of a region rich in history, culture, and

Chapter 11: Practical Information for Travelers Visiting Padua

Planning a trip to Padua involves more than just deciding which historical landmarks or charming streets to explore. From knowing when to visit to understanding the city's public transportation system, cultural etiquette, and the benefits of local tourist passes, there are plenty of practical details that can make your trip smoother and more enjoyable. This guide is designed to provide you with all the essential information you need to confidently navigate Padua like a seasoned traveler. Let's dive into the key details that will help you make the most of your visit.

Best Time to Visit Padua: Weather Guide

Padua, located in northern Italy's Veneto region, enjoys a mild climate but experiences distinct seasons. Choosing the best time to visit depends on your preferences for weather, crowd levels, and seasonal events.

Overview of Padua's Climate

- **Spring (March-May)**: Mild temperatures, blooming flowers, and fewer crowds make this an ideal time to explore the city.
- **Summer (June-August)**: Warm to hot, with average highs reaching 30°C (86°F). Popular with tourists but can get crowded and humid.
- **Fall (September-November)**: Cooler and quieter, with the changing colors of autumn adding charm to Padua's parks and canals.
- **Winter (December-February)**: Cold and damp but festive with holiday markets and fewer tourists. Expect occasional rain and even snow.

Month-by-Month Weather Breakdown

Month	Avg. High (°C)	Avg. Low (°C)	Rainfall (mm)	Daylight Hours
January	6	0	50	9
February	9	1	45	10
March	13	4	60	11
April	17	8	80	13
May	22	13	70	14
June	27	17	60	15
July	30	20	50	15
August	30	19	60	14
September	25	15	70	13
October	18	10	80	11
November	12	5	90	10
December	7	1	60	9

Best Time to Visit: Pros and Cons

- **Spring**: Mild weather, blooming gardens, fewer crowds, and key events like the **Saint Anthony Festival** (June). Ideal for walking tours and outdoor activities.
    - **Pro Tip**: Pack layers for cool mornings and warmer afternoons.
- **Summer**: Long daylight hours and vibrant street life, but prepare for heat, humidity, and larger crowds.
    - **Pro Tip**: Visit early in the morning or later in the afternoon to avoid peak heat and crowds.
- **Fall**: Cooler temperatures, fewer tourists, and beautiful fall foliage. A great time for food and wine festivals.
    - **Pro Tip**: Don't forget a light jacket, as evenings can get chilly.
- **Winter**: Low-season, meaning lower prices and fewer crowds, but be ready for cold, damp conditions.
    - **Pro Tip**: Visit during the holiday season for festive decorations and markets.

Key Takeaway: Spring and fall offer the best balance of pleasant weather and fewer crowds. Summer is perfect if you want to experience Padua at its liveliest, while winter offers a quieter, more intimate look at the city.

Public Transportation: Trams, Buses, and Bicycle Rentals

Padua's public transportation system is well-organized, with efficient trams, buses, and bike rentals, making it easy to get around the city.

Trams and Buses

Padua's tram and bus systems are operated by **APS Mobilità**, providing extensive coverage throughout the city and connecting key sites like **Prato della Valle**, **Piazza dei Signori**, and the **Basilica of Saint Anthony**.

· **Trams**: The **Tram SIR1**line is a modern and eco-friendly option, running from **Guizza**in the south to **Pontevigodarzere** in the north, with stops near major attractions.

· **Buses**: The bus network includes more than 20 lines serving the city and surrounding areas. Buses run frequently, but be aware of limited service on Sundays and holidays.

Ticketing and Validation

- **Tickets**: Tickets can be purchased at **newsstands**, **tabacchi** (tobacco shops), and **automatic machines** at tram stops.
  - **Cost**: A single ticket costs about **€1.30** and is valid for 75 minutes of travel on both buses and trams.
  - **Day Pass**: A 24-hour pass costs around **€4.50**, perfect for unlimited travel in a single day.
- **Validation**: Don't forget to validate your ticket at the yellow machines on trams or buses. Fines for unvalidated tickets can be steep.

Bicycle Rentals

Cycling is a popular and eco-friendly way to explore Padua's flat and bike-friendly streets. The city has dedicated bike lanes and scenic routes along the canals.

- **Where to Rent**:
  - **La Bicicletta Verde**: A popular bike rental shop near **Piazza della Frutta**.
  - **Bike Sharing**: Padua also has a **bike-sharing system**, with pick-up and drop-off points throughout the city.
- **Cost**: Bike rentals start at around **€10 per day**, with lower rates for hourly rentals.

Cycling Tips

- **Safety**: Helmets aren't mandatory but are recommended. Stick to bike lanes where possible, and be mindful of traffic in the city center.
- **Scenic Routes**: Try cycling along the **Naviglio Interno** canal or through **Prato della Valle** for a leisurely ride.

Apps and Online Resources

- **Muoversi in Veneto**: A handy app for real-time information on public transportation routes and schedules.
- **Google Maps**: Provides accurate directions and transit information for trams and buses.

Key Takeaway: Padua's public transportation system is easy to navigate and has affordable ticket options. For a more adventurous way to explore, rent a bike and take advantage of the city's many cycling paths.

Tourist Passes: The Padova Card

If you plan to visit multiple attractions, the **Padova Card offers** excellent value by bundling entrance fees and transportation into one convenient package.

What is the Padova Card?

The **Padova Card** is a tourist pass that grants access to a variety of the city's top attractions, including:

- **Scrovegni Chapel**: One of Padua's most famous sites, with stunning frescoes by Giotto.
- **Basilica of Saint Anthony**: Free entry to the Basilica and nearby **Oratory of San Giorgio**.
- **Museo degli Eremitani**: Featuring archaeology and art collections.

The card also includes **free use of public transportation**(trams and buses) within the city.

Card Options and Prices

- **48-Hour Padova Card**: €16
- **72-Hour Padova Card**: €21

How to Purchase and Use the Card

You can purchase the **Padova Card** online or at tourist offices throughout the city. Once purchased, the card can be activated upon your first use at any attraction or tram/bus ride, and it remains valid for the designated period (48 or 72 hours).

- **Where to Buy**: Available at tourist offices, participating attractions, and online.

Is It Worth It?

The **Padova Card** is an excellent deal if you plan to visit multiple attractions. For example, entrance to the **Scrovegni Chapel** alone costs €14; so with a few more attractions and public transport use, the card quickly pays for itself.

Maximizing the Value of the Card

- **Plan Ahead**: To make the most of your Padova Card, plan your itinerary to visit as many included attractions as possible within the 48 or 72-hour period.
- **Free Transportation**: Don't forget to use the card for public transport—it's a great way to save on getting around the city.

Key Takeaway: If you're planning to explore several of Padua's key attractions, the **Padova Card** offers convenience and savings, especially if you use public transportation.

Understanding Local Customs and Etiquette

It's important to understand and respect local customs when traveling in Padua. Here's a guide to help you navigate social norms, dining etiquette, and cultural practices in the city.

Social Interactions and Greetings

·   **Greetings**: Italians typically greet each other with a friendly **"Buongiorno"** (good morning) or **"Buonasera"** (good evening), depending on the time of day. When meeting someone for the first time, a handshake is common, while friends and family often exchange cheek kisses (starting with the right cheek).

·   **Personal Space**: Italians are generally warm and expressive, and they may stand closer than what some travelers are used to. Don't be surprised if hand gestures accompany conversations.

Dining Customs and Tipping

·   **Meal Times**: Lunch is typically served from 12:30 PM to 2:30 PM, while dinner is later, usually starting around 7:30 PM or 8:00 PM.

·   **Tipping**: Tipping is not obligatory in Italy, as service charges are often included in the bill (noted as "coperto"). However, it's common to leave small changes or round up the bill as a gesture of appreciation.

·   **Dining Etiquette**: When dining, it's polite to wait until everyone's food has arrived before starting your meal. Italians also tend to enjoy leisurely meals, so take your time.

Behavior in Religious Sites

Padua is home to many important religious sites, such as the **Basilica of Saint Anthony**. When visiting these sacred places, it's important to dress modestly and behave respectfully.

- **Dress Code**: Ensure your shoulders and knees are covered when entering churches.
- **Quiet Respect**: Keep your voice low and avoid taking photos in areas where it is not permitted.

Language Tips

While many people in Padua speak English, learning a few basic Italian phrases will go a long way in enhancing your experience.

- **Basic Phrases**:
  - **Hello/Goodbye**: Ciao (informal), Buongiorno/Buonasera (formal)
  - **Please/Thank You**: Per favore / Grazie
  - **Excuse Me/Sorry**: Mi scusi / Scusa
  - **How much does this cost?**: Quanto costa?

Local Customs to Know

· **Coffee Culture**: In Padua, coffee is an art form. Italians typically drink **espresso standing** at the bar rather than sitting down. **Cappuccino** is reserved for mornings, and it's considered odd to order one after lunch.

· **Quiet Time**: Many shops and businesses close during the afternoon, typically from 1:00 PM to 4:00 PM for **riposo**(rest), so plan accordingly.

Key Takeaway:

- Respect local customs.
- Be mindful of dining and religious etiquette.
- Try to learn a few Italian phrases to enhance your experience in Padua.

Responsible Tourism in Padua

As a visitor, it's important to travel responsibly by respecting local communities and minimizing your environmental impact. Here are a few ways you can practice sustainable tourism in Padua:

·   **Support Local Businesses**: Buy from small shops, markets, and family-owned restaurants to support the local economy.

·   **Minimize Waste**: Use refillable water bottles and avoid single-use plastics.

·   **Respect Historical Sites**: Be mindful of the impact you have on historical sites and natural spaces. Follow posted signs and avoid touching delicate structures or artifacts.

Padua is a city of rich history, culture, and natural beauty. By following local customs and traveling responsibly, you'll ensure that your visit not only enhances your experience but also supports the preservation of this incredible destination for future travelers.

Chapter 12: Hidden Gems of Padua

Uncovering the City's Lesser-Known Treasures

While Padua is famous for its grand sights like the **Scrovegni Chapel** and **Basilica of Saint Anthony**, the city holds many lesser-known secrets for curious travelers. Tucked away in quiet corners, these hidden gems offer a glimpse into Padua's rich and varied history, from its Roman origins to its vibrant Jewish community and from forgotten chapels to ancient ruins. Let's embark on a journey through Padua's most intriguing yet often overlooked spots: the **Jewish Ghetto**, **Roman Ruins**, and **Lesser-Known Churches and Chapels**.

Jewish Ghetto: A Quiet Piece of History

A Hidden World Within Padua

Wander into the narrow streets and alleys of **Via San Martino e Solferino**, and you'll find yourself stepping into one of Padua's most historically rich but understated areas: the **Jewish Ghetto**. Although easy to miss, the atmosphere here is distinct from the rest of the bustling city. With its winding lanes, small courtyards, and hidden doorways, the former Jewish Ghetto feels like a world frozen in time. It's quieter than the nearby **Piazza delle Erbe**, offering a peaceful respite and a chance to reflect on the complex history of Padua's Jewish community.

A Brief History of Padua's Jewish Community

The Jewish community in Padua dates back to the **11th century**, and it is one of the oldest in Italy. During the Renaissance, Padua became a significant center of Jewish learning, with the **University of Padua** allowing Jewish students to study medicine and philosophy. However, like many other cities in Italy, the Jewish population was confined to a ghetto starting in **1603**, isolated from the rest of the city by walls and gates that were locked at night.

Despite these restrictions, the Jewish community thrived within these boundaries, contributing significantly to Padua's cultural and intellectual life.

Key Points of Interest in the Ghetto

·   **The Synagogue**: One of the few remaining synagogues in Padua, **Sinagoga Italiana**, is located on **Via delle Piazze**. While the original structure has been rebuilt due to fire damage, it remains a symbol of the Jewish presence in the city. Today, it is still used for religious services, and visitors can arrange guided tours to explore its interior.

·   **Jewish Cemetery**: Another important site is the **Jewish Cemetery Via Wiel**, one of the oldest in Europe. Wandering through the gravestones, you'll find inscriptions in Hebrew, a poignant reminder of the centuries-old Jewish community.

·   **Architectural Features**: As you explore the area, take note of the narrow windows and small balconies that mark the buildings as typical ghetto architecture. Many of these structures have been carefully preserved, allowing visitors to imagine what life was like in the confined quarters.

Suggested Walking Route

Begin your walk at **Via San Martino e Solferino**, then wander down **Via delle Piazze** to admire the **Sinagoga Italiana**. From there, explore the nearby **Via Marsala**, where you can feel the echoes of history in the quiet alleyways. End your walk at the **Jewish Cemetery** for a reflective moment in this peaceful, historic space.

Tips for Exploring

- **Respectful Exploration**: The Jewish Ghetto remains a quiet residential area, so explore respectfully. Keep noise levels low, and be mindful when taking photos.
- **Guided Tours**: For a deeper understanding of the area, consider joining a tour focused on **Padua's Jewish history**. Local guides can offer fascinating insights and stories you might otherwise miss.

Local Insight: During the ghetto era, gates were locked every evening, and Jews were required to wear identifying badges. Despite these restrictions, Padua's Jewish community became renowned for its scholars and physicians, many of whom were respected across Europe.

Intriguing Fact: Padua's **Jewish cemetery** contains tombstones dating back to the 16th century, making it one of the oldest Jewish burial grounds in the region.

Roman Ruins: Discovering Padua's Ancient Past

Padua's Roman Origins

Long before it became a medieval powerhouse, Padua was a thriving Roman settlement known as **Patavium**. Established in the 4th century BCE, the city became one of the wealthiest in northern Italy, famed for its wool production and strategic location along trade routes. Although much of Roman Padua lies buried beneath modern streets, you can still discover traces of this ancient past in a few key locations around the city.

Significant Roman Remains

· **Arena Gardens and Roman Amphitheater**

The **Arena Gardens** (Giardini dell'Arena) offer a peaceful green space in the heart of the city, but hidden within is one of Padua's most impressive Roman relics: the remains of a **Roman amphitheater**. While only parts of the original structure are visible, this site once held gladiatorial contests and public spectacles. The nearby **Scrovegni Chapel** was actually built on the ruins of this amphitheater, and if you look closely, you can still see the outline of the Roman structure.

·   **Roman Bridge at Ponte San Lorenzo**

Hidden beneath modern-day **Ponte San Lorenzo**, a busy street in the city center, are the remains of a **Roman bridge**. While much of the bridge is now submerged, a small section has been excavated and is visible through glass panels installed in the pavement above. This bridge once spanned the **Medoacus River**, a vital waterway during the Roman era.

·   **Via Tadi Ruins**

Along **Via Tadi**, you'll find the remnants of **Roman walls** that once encircled the city. These walls, though modest in appearance today, were part of the fortifications that protected ancient Patavium from invaders.

Understanding Padua's Roman Past

While the ruins are somewhat scattered and less prominent than those in Rome or Verona, they offer a fascinating glimpse into Padua's Roman history. The city was a key player in the Roman Republic and later the Empire, contributing to the region's economy and culture.

Practical Information and Tips

- **How to Visit**: The **Arena Gardens** are free to enter, and the Roman amphitheater remains are easy to spot. The **Ponte San Lorenzo** ruins can be viewed from the street, but keep an eye out for the glass panels as they can be easy to miss.

- **Nearby Sites**: For a more comprehensive understanding of Padua's ancient history, visit the **Museo Archeologico** at **Palazzo degli Eremitani**, which houses artifacts from the city's Roman era.

Local Insight: During its Roman heyday, **Patavium was** one of the most prosperous cities in northern Italy, known for its extensive wool trade. In fact, ancient historians often praised Padua for its wealth and civic pride.

Intriguing Fact: The Roman amphitheater in Padua was built to rival those in larger cities. However, much of it was dismantled during the Middle Ages to repurpose its stones for other buildings.

Lesser-Known Churches and Chapels: Spiritual Treasures Off the Beaten Path

A Different Side of Padua's Religious Heritage

While the **Basilica of Saint Anthony and Scrovegni Chapel** are undoubtedly Padua's most famous religious sites, the city is also home to a number of lesser-known churches and chapels that boast incredible art, architecture, and history. These hidden spiritual treasures offer a quieter, more intimate glimpse into the city's religious life.

Hidden Church Gems in Padua

- **Chiesa di San Gaetano**

Nestled on **Via Altinate**, this Baroque church is a masterpiece of 17th-century architecture. Its ornate interior is filled with gilded altars, frescoed ceilings, and intricate stucco work. Despite its grandeur, **Chiesa di San Gaetano** is often overlooked by visitors, making it a peaceful spot for quiet contemplation.

- **Oratorio di San Michele**

Tucked away near **Ponte Molino**, this small but beautifully frescoed chapel dates back to the 11th century. The **Oratorio di San Michele** is famous for its **14th-century frescoes** depicting scenes from the life of the Virgin Mary. Though lesser-known than the frescoes in the Scrovegni Chapel, these artworks are equally captivating in their detail and color.

- **Chiesa di Santa Sofia**

One of the oldest churches in Padua, **Chiesa di Santa Sofia**stands out for its unusual architectural style, blending early Christian and Byzantine influences. Its simple, austere exterior contrasts with the intricate columns and arches inside, making it a fascinating study of architectural evolution.

- **Chiesa di San Daniele**

Located in the quiet **San Daniele** district, this small church houses a beautiful collection of Renaissance frescoes. The serene atmosphere and lack of crowds make it the perfect place to escape the busier tourist sites.

Suggested Route for Visiting

Start at **Chiesa di San Gaetano** and make your way to the **Oratorio di San Michele**. From there, head toward **Chiesa di Santa Sofia** for a look at one of Padua's most ancient religious buildings. End your tour at **Chiesa di San Daniele** for a peaceful moment in one of Padua's quietest corners.

Tips for Visiting

Etiquette: As these are still functioning churches, it's important to dress modestly (covering shoulders and knees) and be mindful of any ongoing services. Quiet, respectful behavior is expected.

Best Times to Visit: Mornings are ideal for visiting these churches, as they are often quieter and allow for a more reflective experience.

Local Insight: **Chiesa di Santa Sofia has** been standing since the 10th century and is believed to have been built on the site of a Roman temple, reflecting the city's layers of history.

Intriguing Fact: The **Oratorio di San Michele** survived centuries of floods and earthquakes, yet its frescoes remain remarkably well-preserved, offering visitors a vivid glimpse into medieval religious art.

While Padua is known for its major landmarks, its hidden gems offer a different kind of magic. From the quiet alleys of the **Jewish Ghetto to** the ancient **Roman ruins** and forgotten **churches**, these sites provide a deeper understanding of the city's rich and complex history. Whether you're wandering through medieval streets or discovering hidden frescoes, these lesser-known corners of Padua will leave you with a sense of wonder and connection to the past.

As you explore these hidden gems, remember to travel respectfully. Many of these sites are still used by locals for religious or personal purposes, so be mindful of your impact. Keep noise to a minimum, follow any guidelines posted at the sites, and leave no trace behind to help preserve these historical treasures for future generations.

Chapter 13: Safety, Health, and Travel Tips for Visitors to Padua

Padua, with its rich history and vibrant culture, is a delightful destination that promises a safe and enjoyable experience for travelers. However, like any travel destination, it's important to be prepared and informed to ensure a smooth trip. This section provides comprehensive guidance on staying safe and healthy during your visit to Padua, covering essential emergency contacts, practical health and safety tips, and advice on travel insurance and accessing healthcare services. With a balanced approach, we aim to equip you with the knowledge you need to confidently explore Padua while taking common-sense precautions.

Health and Safety: Emergency Contacts and Tips

Essential Emergency Numbers

In the unlikely event of an emergency, having the right contact information at your fingertips can make a big difference. Here are the key numbers you should keep handy during your stay in Padua:

- **Police**: 112 (General emergencies, including police, ambulance, and fire)
- **Ambulance**: 118 (For medical emergencies requiring immediate assistance)
- **Fire Department**: 115
- **Tourist Police**: 113 (Dedicated to helping tourists with safety and legal issues)
- **24-Hour Pharmacies**: Look for signs saying "Farmacia" with a green cross. The main 24-hour pharmacy in Padua is **Farmacia Centrale**, located at **Piazza delle Erbe 9**.
- **Hospitals with Emergency Services**:
    - **Ospedale di Padova** (Via Giustiniani, 2) - the main hospital with comprehensive emergency services.

- **Policlinico Universitario** (Via Giustiniani, 2) - particularly known for specialized care.

Safety Tip: Always carry a copy of your ID and emergency contact numbers with you, especially when exploring unfamiliar areas.

General Health Tips for Travelers
- **Food and Water Safety**: Padua's food and water quality are generally excellent, but it's always wise to stick to bottled water if you have a sensitive stomach. Enjoy local delicacies, but ensure that food is cooked thoroughly, especially seafood and street food.
- **Sun Protection and Heat**: Padua can get quite warm in summer. Protect yourself from the sun by wearing sunscreen, a hat, and sunglasses, and stay hydrated throughout the day.
- **Specific Health Concerns**: There are no specific health concerns unique to Padua, but as with any travel, it's wise to have up-to-date vaccinations for tetanus, measles, mumps, rubella, and influenza.

Accessing Medical Care as a Tourist

Padua offers high-quality medical care, and tourists can access services at both public and private facilities. Most medical staff, especially in hospitals, speak basic English, though it's helpful to have a translation app or phrasebook for less common conditions.

- **Local Health Apps**: Consider downloading the **official app of the Italian Ministry of Health**, which provides information on nearby healthcare facilities and pharmacies. It also offers guidance on what to do in case of specific health emergencies.

Key Takeaway: Familiarize yourself with the location of the nearest hospital and pharmacy to your accommodation, and don't hesitate to ask locals or your hotel for recommendations on healthcare services if needed.

Staying Safe in Padua: Local Advice
Overview of Padua's Safety Situation

Padua is generally a safe city, with a low crime rate and friendly locals. Like many European cities, it's vibrant and lively, especially in popular tourist areas. However, as with any travel destination, it's important to remain vigilant and take standard safety precautions.

Specific Safety Tips

- **Navigating the City, Especially at Night**: Padua's historic center is generally safe to explore day and night, but it's advisable to stick to well-lit, busy areas after dark. Avoid poorly lit parks or alleyways, particularly in less busy neighborhoods outside the city center.
- **Using Public Transportation Safely**: Public transportation in Padua, including buses and trams, is safe and reliable. Keep an eye on your belongings, especially during rush hours when buses and trams can be crowded.
- **Protecting Belongings from Pickpockets**: Pickpocketing can occur in busy areas, such as markets or popular tourist sites. Use a crossbody bag or a money belt to keep valuables secure, and avoid displaying expensive items like jewelry or large amounts of cash.
- **Avoiding Common Tourist Scams**: Be wary of overly friendly strangers offering unsolicited help, especially at ATMs or ticket machines. If someone tries to distract you or asks for money in an unusual situation, it's best to walk away.

Areas to Be Extra Cautious In

While Padua is generally safe, exercise caution around the **Padua Train Station**, especially late at night. Like in many cities, train stations can attract opportunistic individuals, so keep your belongings close and be mindful of your surroundings.

Respecting Local Laws and Customs

- **Public Drinking**: While enjoying a spritz on a terrace is a beloved local pastime, drinking alcohol in public streets or parks can be frowned upon and, in some areas, is subject to fines.
- **Dress Modestly in Churches**: When visiting churches or religious sites, dress modestly by covering shoulders and knees. This shows respect for local customs and religious practices.

Tips for Solo Travelers, Especially Women

- **Stay in Central Areas**: Opt for accommodations in central, well-reviewed neighborhoods like **Centro Storico** or **Santa Sofia**. These areas are well-lit and have more pedestrian traffic.
- **Stay Connected**: Share your itinerary with someone back home, and keep your phone charged and accessible. Local SIM cards or portable Wi-Fi devices can help you stay connected throughout your trip.

Local Insight: Padua has active community policing and several local initiatives aimed at maintaining the city's safety, including increased patrols in tourist-heavy areas.

Key Takeaway: Padua is a welcoming and safe city for travelers. With a bit of common sense and awareness, you can enjoy your time here without worry.

Travel Insurance and Health Services

The Importance of Travel Insurance

Travel insurance is an essential part of your planning for a trip to Padua. It provides peace of mind and financial protection in case of unexpected situations such as medical emergencies, trip cancellations, or lost luggage.

What Good Travel Insurance Should Cover?

- **Medical Coverage**: Ensure your insurance covers emergency medical treatment, hospital stays, and, if necessary, medical evacuation. Given the high quality of healthcare in Italy, costs can be substantial without insurance.
- **Trip Cancellation and Interruption**: Look for policies that reimburse you for cancellations due to illness, family emergencies, or unforeseen events like natural disasters.
- **Baggage and Personal Belongings**: Coverage for lost, stolen, or damaged baggage is crucial, especially if you're traveling with valuable items.
- **Personal Liability**: This covers you in case you accidentally cause harm to someone else or damage property.

Tips for Choosing the Right Travel Insurance

- **Compare Policies**: Use comparison websites to evaluate different plans and ensure they meet your needs. Consider factors such as deductible amounts, coverage limits, and specific exclusions.
- **Read the Fine Print**: Understand what is and isn't covered, including any specific activities (like hiking or sports) you plan to do in Padua.

The Healthcare System in Padua

Padua's healthcare system is part of the broader Italian healthcare network, which is known for its high standards and accessibility. Tourists can receive care at public hospitals, and emergency services are available to everyone, regardless of nationality.

- **Accessing Medical Services as a Tourist**: In an emergency, you can visit any public hospital or clinic. Bring your passport and travel insurance details. Non-emergency care, such as doctor visits or prescriptions, may incur fees, which you should be prepared to pay upfront and claim back from your insurer.
- **Quality and Cost**: Healthcare in Padua is of high quality, but costs can vary. Private services are typically more expensive but may offer shorter wait times and English-speaking staff.
- **Reciprocal Healthcare Agreements**: EU citizens should bring their **European Health Insurance Card (EHIC)**, which provides access to necessary healthcare under the same conditions as local residents. Check if your country has a reciprocal healthcare agreement with Italy for similar benefits.

Pharmacies and Obtaining Prescription Medications

- **Pharmacies** (Farmacie) are widespread in Padua, with many offering extended hours and some open 24 hours. For minor ailments, pharmacists can provide advice and over-the-counter medications.
- **Prescriptions**: If you need prescription medication, bring a copy of your prescription or a note from your doctor. Italian pharmacists can often provide equivalent medications, but having documentation helps avoid any confusion.

Vaccinations and Health Preparations

No specific vaccinations are required for visiting Padua, but it's wise to ensure standard vaccines (tetanus, diphtheria, hepatitis A and B) are up-to-date. Consider travel health insurance that covers the cost of any unexpected vaccines.

Safety Tip: Always keep a basic first-aid kit and any necessary medications with you, especially if you have known allergies or conditions that require specific treatments.

Key Takeaway: Travel insurance is your best safeguard against the unexpected. Ensure your policy covers medical emergencies and familiarize yourself with local healthcare facilities to ensure a worry-free visit.

Final Thoughts on Safety: Be Informed and Prepared

While Padua is generally a safe and welcoming city, being prepared and aware of local health and safety resources is crucial to ensuring a smooth trip. Stay informed about current events, and check your government's travel advisories before and during your trip. Remember, the key to a great travel experience is balancing the joy of exploration with a little proactive planning and care.

Enjoy your journey to Padua, stay safe, and make the most of everything this charming city has to offer!

FAQ for Visitors to Padua

Planning a trip to Padua? This FAQ section aims to provide you with essential, practical information to help you make the most of your visit. From travel tips to language basics and currency and tipping etiquette, we've got you covered with everything you need to know for a smooth and enjoyable trip.

Common Questions About Visiting Padua

1. What's the best way to get to Padua from major Italian cities?

- **From Venice:** Padua is just a 30-minute train ride from Venice. High-speed trains run frequently, making this the quickest and most convenient option.
- **From Milan:** You can reach Padua in about 2 hours by taking a high-speed train. Trains depart regularly from Milano Centrale station.

- **From Rome:** High-speed trains connect Rome and Padua in approximately 3-4 hours. Look for trains departing from Roma Termini station.

Pro Tip: Book train tickets in advance to secure the best prices and avoid last-minute hassles. Websites like Trenitalia or Italo offer easy online booking.

2. How many days should I spend in Padua?

To fully experience Padua's charm, a stay of 2-3 days is ideal. This allows enough time to explore the city's highlights, enjoy local cuisine, and soak in the relaxed atmosphere. If you have more time, consider taking day trips to nearby destinations like Venice or Verona.

3. What are the must-see attractions in Padua?

- **Scrovegni Chapel:** Famous for Giotto's stunning frescoes, this is a must-see for art lovers.
- **Prato della Valle:** One of the largest squares in Europe, perfect for a stroll.
- **Basilica of Saint Anthony:** A major pilgrimage site with beautiful architecture and religious significance.
- **Botanical Garden:** The world's oldest academic botanical garden, a UNESCO World Heritage Site.
- **Palazzo della Ragione:** A historic marketplace with a fascinating frescoed hall.

4. Is Padua expensive compared to other Italian cities?

Padua is generally more affordable than major tourist hotspots like Venice, Florence, or Rome. Accommodation, dining, and attractions are reasonably priced, making it a great destination for budget-conscious travelers.

5. What's the best area to stay in Padua?

- **Centro Storico (Historic Center):** Ideal for first-time visitors, offering proximity to major attractions, restaurants, and shops.

- **Santa Croce:** A quieter residential area, perfect for families or those seeking a more relaxed stay.
- **Prato della Valle:** Close to parks and gardens, with easy access to the city's main sights.

Pro Tip: Check accommodation reviews on platforms like Booking.com or Airbnb to find a place that suits your needs and preferences.

6. Are credit cards widely accepted in Padua?

Credit cards are widely accepted in Padua, especially in hotels, restaurants, and larger shops. However, some smaller establishments, cafes, and market stalls may only accept cash. It's always good to carry some euros for small purchases.

7. Is Padua suitable for family, solo, or budget travel?

- **Family Travel:** Padua is family-friendly, with plenty of parks, pedestrian areas, and kid-friendly attractions like the Botanical Garden and local museums.
- **Solo Travel:** Padua is safe for solo travelers, with a welcoming vibe and plenty of things to do. Solo travelers will appreciate the city's walkability and vibrant café culture.
- **Budget Travel:** With reasonably priced accommodations, affordable eateries, and free or low-cost attractions, Padua is perfect for budget travelers.

Key Takeaway: Padua is a versatile destination that caters to various travel styles. It is a perfect choice for anyone looking to explore an authentic Italian city without the overwhelming crowds of more touristy locations.

Language Tips: Basic Italian Phrases for Tourists
The Importance of Knowing Some Basic Italian

While many Italians in Padua speak English, especially in tourist areas, learning a few basic Italian phrases can greatly enhance your experience. Locals appreciate the effort, and it can help you navigate more smoothly, especially in shops, restaurants, or when asking for directions.

Here's a handy table of essential phrases to help you get started:

Italian Phrase	Phonetic Pronunciation	English Translation
Ciao	[chow]	Hello/Goodbye
Buongiorno	[bwon-jor-no]	Good morning
Buonasera	[bwon-a-se-ra]	Good evening
Per favore	[per fa-vo-re]	Please
Grazie	[gra-zee-eh]	Thank you
Mi scusi	[mee skoo-zee]	Excuse me
Dov'è...?	[doh-veh]	Where is...?
Quanto costa?	[kwan-to koh-sta]	How much does it cost?
Il conto, per favore	[eel kon-to per fa-vo-re]	The bill, please
Parla inglese?	[par-la een-gleh-zeh]	Do you speak English?
Non capisco	[non ka-pee-sko]	I don't understand
Acqua	[ah-kwa]	Water
Numero	[noo-meh-ro]	Number
Aiuto!	[ah-yoo-toh]	Help!

Pro Tip: When speaking Italian, pronounce each vowel distinctly and avoid rushing through words. Italians also use hand gestures frequently to emphasize their words, so don't be shy about using them—it's part of the local charm!

Tips on Italian Pronunciation and Gestures

- **Pronunciation:** Italian is largely phonetic. Each letter (especially vowels) is pronounced clearly, and words often end in vowels.

- **Gestures:** Italians are known for expressive gestures. A friendly wave of the hand is often used for greetings, and a slight nod of the head can be a subtle way to say "yes."

Key Takeaway: Even a few basic phrases can make a big difference in how you experience Padua. Embrace the language, even if it's just a few words—locals will appreciate your effort, and it will add a layer of enjoyment to your travel.

Currency and Tipping Etiquette in Italy

Overview of the Euro and Its Denominations

Italy uses the Euro (€). Here's a quick guide to the denominations:
- **Coins:** 1, 2, 5, 10, 20, 50 cents; €1, €2
- **Banknotes:** €5, €10, €20, €50, €100, €200, €500

Pro Tip: Always carry a mix of small bills and coins for minor purchases or when paying in cash-only establishments.

Currency Exchange and ATMs

- **Where to Exchange Currency:** Currency exchange services are available at airports, major train stations, and some banks. However, rates can be less favorable compared to using ATMs.
- **Using ATMs in Padua:** ATMs (called "Bancomat") are widely available and offer a convenient way to withdraw euros. They generally provide good exchange rates, though your home bank may charge a foreign transaction fee.
- **Credit Card Acceptance:** Credit cards are widely accepted, but always check for potential foreign transaction fees with your card provider. Visa and Mastercard are the most commonly accepted cards.

Pro Tip: Notify your bank before traveling to avoid any blocks on your card due to unusual activity.

Tipping Customs in Italy

Tipping in Italy is less common than in some other countries, and it's not obligatory. However, a small tip is appreciated for good service. Here's a quick guide:

- **Restaurants and Cafes:** A service charge (servizio) is often included in your bill, usually around 10-15%. If it's not included, a tip of 5-10% is appreciated for good service. Leaving a few euros or rounding up the bill is also common.
- **Bars and Coffee Shops:** Tipping is not expected, but you can leave small change (10-20 cents) if you feel the service was exceptional.
- **Taxis:** Rounding up to the nearest euro or adding 5-10% is appreciated but not required.
- **Hotels:** It's polite to tip porters (€1-2 per bag) and housekeeping (€1-2 per day).
- **Tour Guides:** For guided tours, tipping €5-10 per person is a nice gesture for excellent service.

Handling Bills and Checking for Hidden Charges

Always check your bill for any added charges. Common additions might include:

- **Pane e Coperto:** A small charge for bread and cover, typically €1-3 per person.
- **Service Charge:** If already included, you are not expected to tip further unless you wish to.

Key Takeaway: Tipping in Italy is more of a gesture of appreciation than an obligation. Focus on enjoying your meal or service, and tip according to the level of satisfaction rather than out of necessity.

Traveling to Padua is an enriching experience that offers a unique blend of history, art, and Italian charm. By familiarizing yourself with basic Italian phrases, understanding currency and tipping customs, and knowing what to expect, you'll be well-prepared to make the most of your visit. Don't hesitate to embrace local customs, and remember that a warm smile and a friendly "Grazie" go a long way in making connections and enjoying your time in this beautiful city.

Stay Informed: Always keep an eye on current events and check your government's travel advisories before and during your trip. Padua is generally a safe and welcoming destination, but being prepared and informed is the key to a smooth travel experience.

Safe travels, and enjoy your adventure in Padua!

Conclusion

Padua, often overshadowed by its more famous neighbors Venice and Verona, is a city of immense historical depth, vibrant culture, and hidden gems waiting to be discovered. From its ancient Roman roots to its medieval grandeur and Renaissance artistry, Padua offers a tapestry of experiences that appeal to travelers of all kinds. In this guide, we've explored many facets of Padua—from its secret spots like the Jewish Ghetto and lesser-known churches to practical tips on navigating the city and ensuring a safe visit. However, as with any historic city, the true essence of Padua is best understood by exploring beyond the obvious, engaging with its local culture, and savoring the unique blend of past and present that defines this captivating city.

A City of Hidden Gems and Rich History

One of the most enchanting aspects of Padua is its ability to surprise and delight v

isitors with its hidden treasures. The Jewish Ghetto, for example, offers a quiet glimpse into the city's layered past. Walking through its narrow streets, visitors can sense the echoes of a community that thrived amidst adversity, leaving behind a legacy of resilience and cultural richness. Whether it's exploring synagogues that have stood the test of time or tracing the stories of notable residents, the Ghetto provides a poignant reminder of Padua's diverse heritage.

Similarly, Padua's Roman ruins serve as tangible connections to its ancient origins. The remnants of the Roman amphitheater and other archaeological sites tell stories of a city that was once a bustling hub of the Roman Empire. These sites, while not as grand as Rome's, offer an intimate, almost personal, glimpse into the daily lives of ancient Paduans. This connection between the past and present is a recurring theme throughout Padua, where layers of history coexist with modern life, creating a unique and compelling narrative for those willing to explore beyond the surface.

The lesser-known churches and chapels of Padua, often overshadowed by the grand Basilica of Saint Anthony, are hidden sanctuaries filled with art, history, and spirituality. These quiet spaces invite reflection and provide insight into the city's religious and artistic heritage. From exquisite frescoes tucked away in small chapels to architectural marvels hidden in plain sight, these sites highlight the intricate beauty that defines Padua's religious landscape.

Practical Tips for Exploring Padua

Navigating Padua's streets, whether on foot, by bike, or via public transport, is a straightforward and enjoyable experience. The city's compact size and pedestrian-friendly layout make it easy to explore its many attractions without the need for extensive planning. A good city center map is an invaluable tool for first-time visitors, offering a clear layout of the main sights and suggesting routes that connect them efficiently. Public transport, with its well-coordinated bus and tram systems, extends the reach of exploration, allowing travelers to venture beyond the city center to discover less touristy areas that are equally rich in charm and history.

For those looking to explore on two wheels, Padua's bike-friendly infrastructure offers a delightful alternative. With numerous cycling paths crisscrossing the city, biking not only provides a convenient mode of transport but also a chance to experience Padua at a leisurely pace. Whether pedaling along the banks of the Bacchiglione River or weaving through historic streets, cycling adds an extra layer of enjoyment to the journey.

Walking, of course, remains one of the best ways to soak in the atmosphere of Padua. From the vibrant markets of Piazza delle Erbe to the tranquil gardens of the University of Padua's Botanical Garden, each step reveals a new facet of the city's character. Walking routes, whether guided by maps or simply following one's instincts, lead to unexpected discoveries—hidden courtyards, charming cafes, and locals going about their daily lives.

Safety, Health, and Responsible Tourism

Padua is generally a safe city, but like any travel destination, a few precautions can go a long way in ensuring a smooth and enjoyable visit. Familiarizing oneself with local emergency contacts, being mindful of personal belongings, and respecting local customs are simple yet effective ways to stay safe. The city's healthcare system is accessible and of high quality, offering peace of mind to travelers who may need medical assistance.

Travel insurance is another essential aspect of trip planning, providing coverage for unexpected events that could disrupt your journey. From medical emergencies to trip cancellations, a good travel insurance policy offers a safety net that allows you to explore Padua with confidence.

Responsible tourism is about more than just following rules; it's about engaging with Padua in a way that respects its heritage and contributes positively to the local community. This includes supporting local businesses, respecting historic sites, and being mindful of environmental impacts. Small actions, such as reducing waste, avoiding single-use plastics, and choosing sustainable transport options, help preserve Padua's beauty for future generations.

Experiencing Padua's Culture and Lifestyle

Beyond its historic sites and attractions, Padua is a city that thrives on its vibrant culture and everyday life. The city's markets are a microcosm of Italian life, bustling with vendors selling fresh produce, local delicacies, and handcrafted goods. Visiting these markets not only offers a chance to sample authentic flavors but also provides a glimpse into the rhythms of daily life in Padua.

Dining in Padua is an experience in itself, with a culinary scene that ranges from traditional trattorias serving regional dishes to contemporary restaurants experimenting with modern twists on classic recipes. Venetian influences are evident in many of the local specialties, from the risottos and polentas to the seafood dishes that celebrate the region's proximity to the coast. Don't miss the chance to try some of Padua's signature dishes, such as **"bigoli in salsa"** (thick spaghetti with a savory anchovy sauce) or **"risotto al tastasal"** (risotto with seasoned pork).

Wine lovers will find Padua to be a gateway to some of Italy's finest vineyards. The nearby Euganean Hills are renowned for their wine production, offering a range of reds, whites, and sparkling wines that reflect the rich terroir of the region. A day trip to these vineyards, complete with tastings and tours, is a perfect way to unwind and savor the flavors of the Veneto.

Padua's cultural calendar is filled with events that celebrate its artistic and intellectual heritage. From music festivals and art exhibitions to theatrical performances and scholarly lectures, the city offers a diverse array of activities that cater to all interests. The University of Padua, one of the oldest and most prestigious universities in the world, continues to be a hub of academic and cultural activity, hosting events that draw scholars and visitors alike.

Embracing Padua's Spirit

At its core, Padua is a city that invites exploration, curiosity, and a willingness to venture off the beaten path. While it boasts famous sites like the Scrovegni Chapel and the Basilica of Saint Anthony, it's the lesser-known corners, the quiet streets, and the local interactions that truly define the Padua experience. The city's charm lies in its authenticity—its ability to balance the grandeur of its history with the simplicity of everyday life.

Whether you're admiring the intricate frescoes of a hidden chapel, savoring a gelato in a sun-drenched piazza, or simply people-watching from a cafe terrace, Padua offers moments of connection that resonate deeply with travelers. It's a city that doesn't demand attention but rather rewards those who take the time to look closer, engage with its stories, and appreciate the layers of history that have shaped its identity.

Final Reflections: Your Journey to Padua

As you prepare for your journey to Padua, remember that the city's greatest treasures often lie beyond the guidebooks. While planning and preparation are important, leaving room for spontaneity and personal discovery is equally valuable. Allow yourself to wander, ask questions, and connect with the locals who call Padua home. Their insights, recommendations, and stories will enrich your experience in ways that no map or guide can.

In the end, Padua is more than just a destination—it's an invitation to slow down, immerse yourself in a rich tapestry of art, culture, and history, and find joy in the simple act of exploring. Whether you're visiting for a few days or an extended stay, Padua's charm will leave a lasting impression, drawing you back to its streets, its stories, and its timeless allure.

Safe travels, and may your time in Padua be filled with discovery, delight, and a deeper connection to this remarkable city. As you uncover its hidden gems and embrace its vibrant spirit, you'll find that Padua is not just a place to visit but a place to experience—and, perhaps, a place to return to time and time again.

Map of Padua

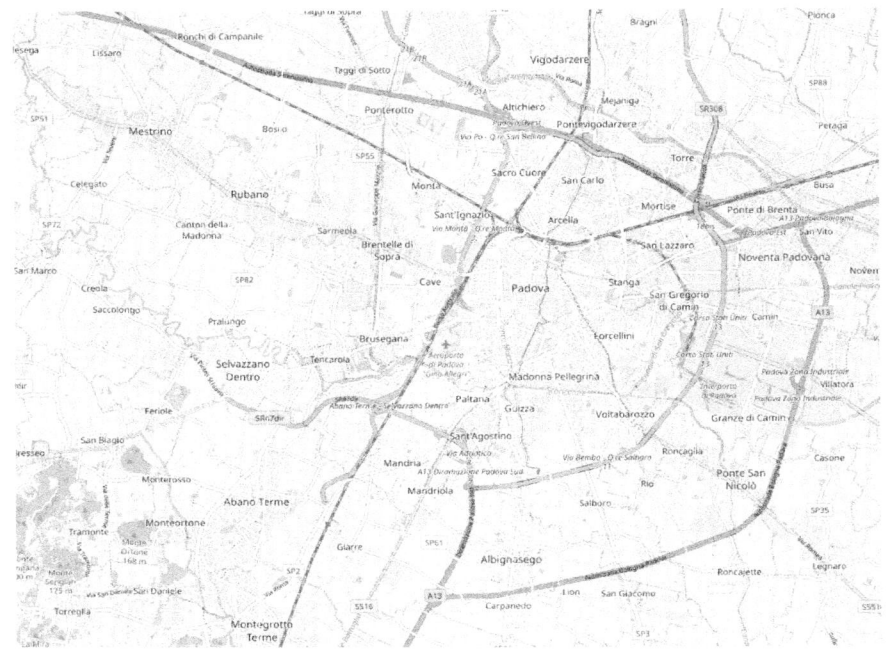

https://www.openstreetmap.org/#map=12/45.3984/11.8481

Map of Cheap Hotels in Padua

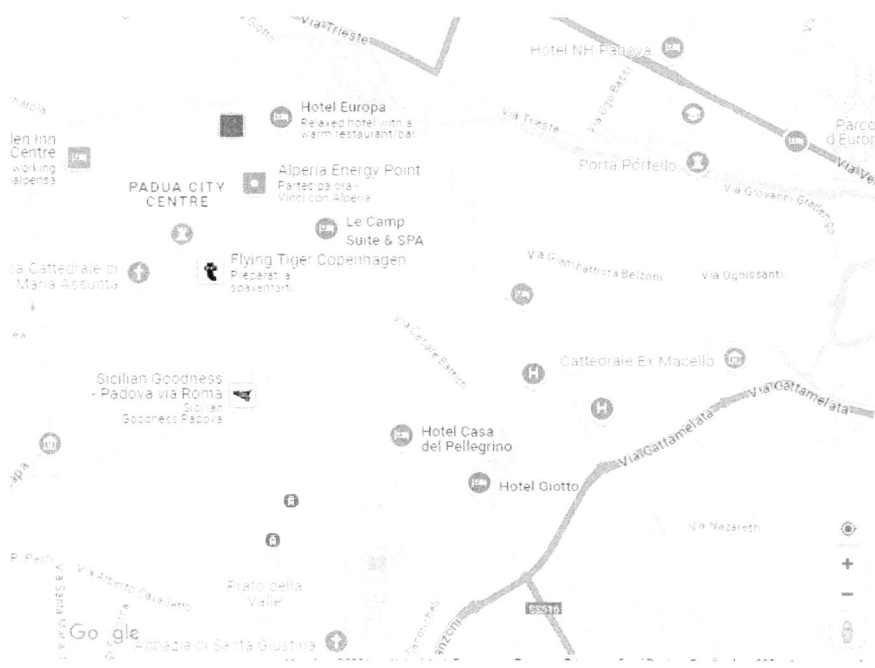

https://maps.app.goo.gl/suDEX77frafrhNnr9

Map of Where to Stay in Padua

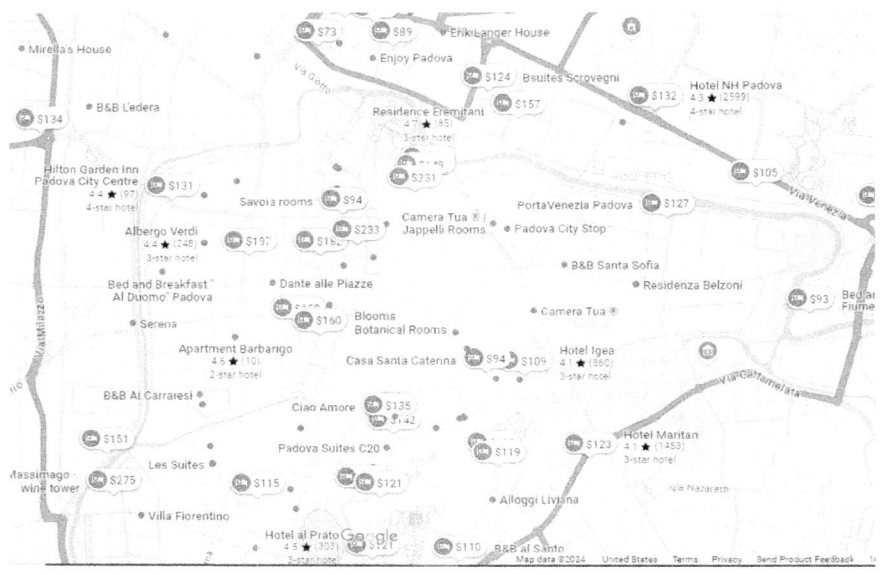

https://maps.app.goo.gl/cpbBFLXoryrTbpgS6

Map of Where to Eat in Padua

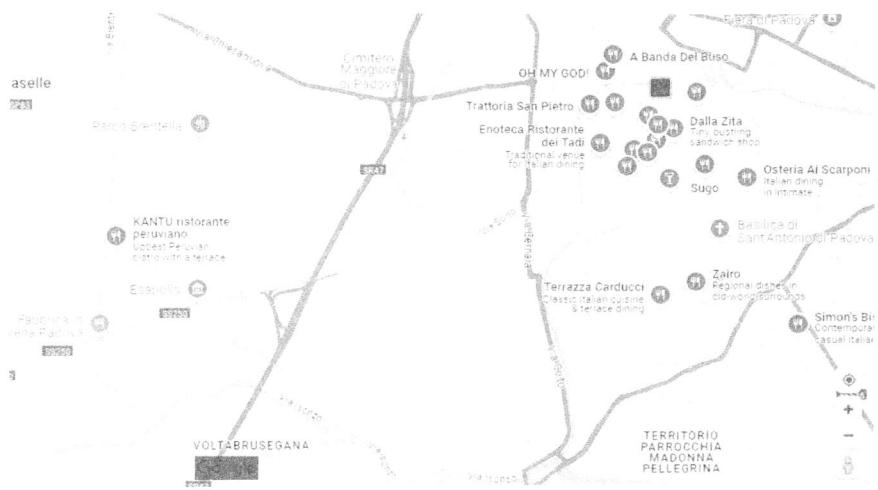

https://maps.app.goo.gl/CYeZNmhqnGQCXf9D9

Map of Beaches near Padua

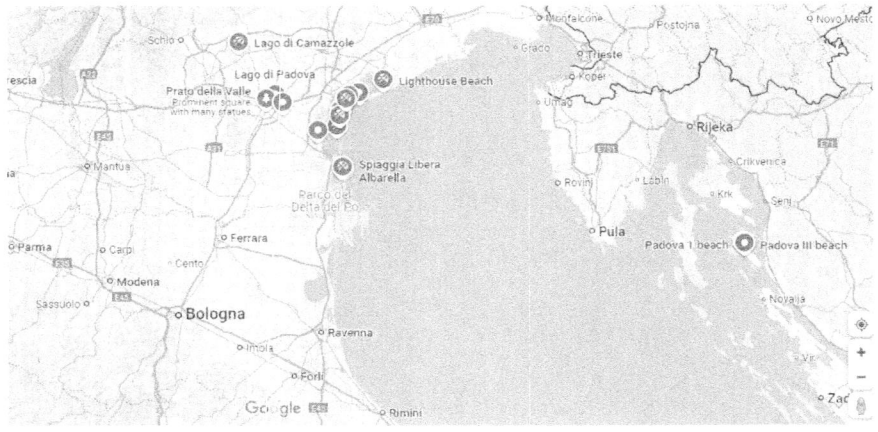

https://maps.app.goo.gl/wht5HFYeMjP3SgiD9

Map of Museums in Padua

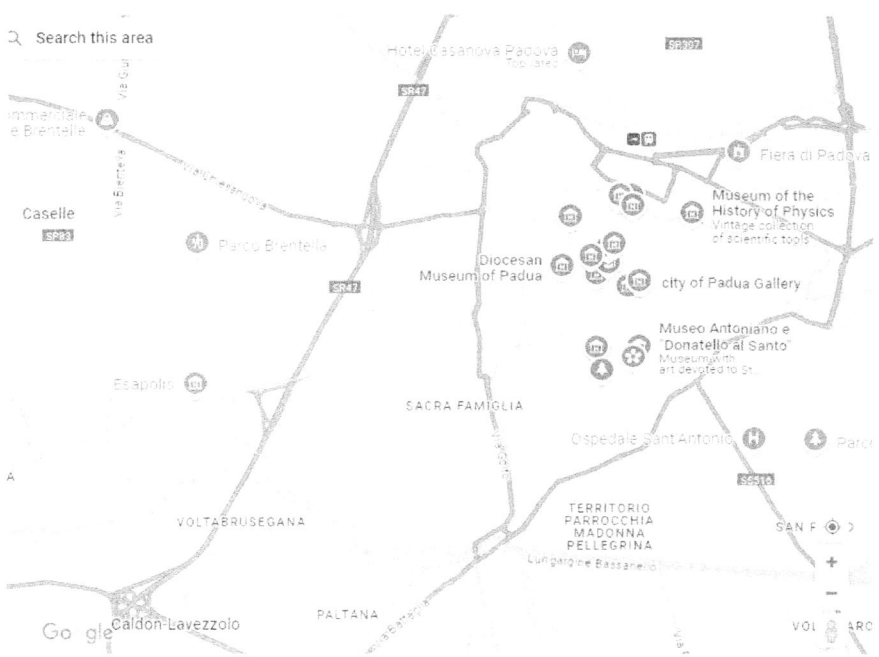

https://maps.app.goo.gl/SQFn2xmuReSsLvTo8

Map of where to Hike in and Around Padua

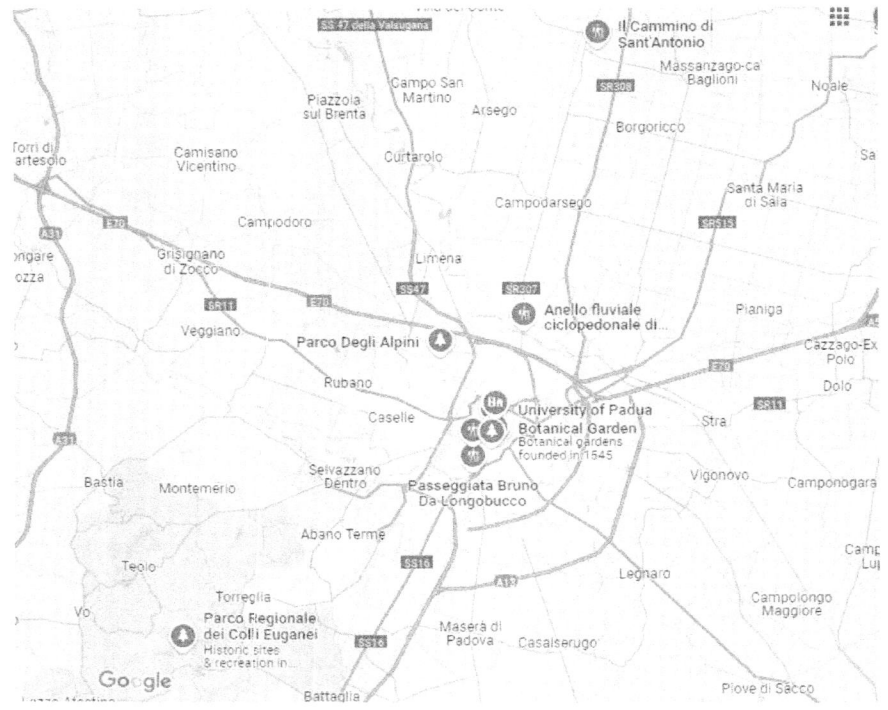

https://maps.app.goo.gl/NWbfpeqCz3JGPj3V7

137

Map of Padua's Historic sites

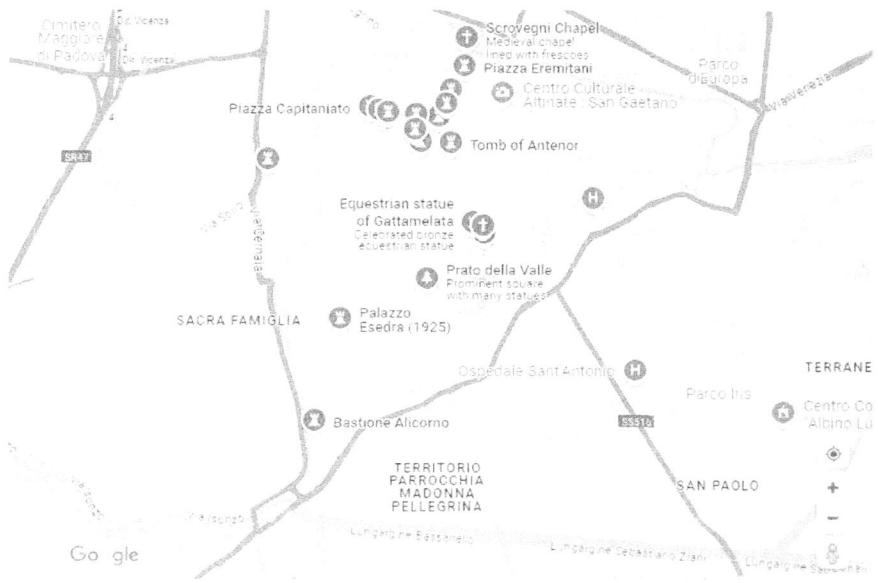

https://maps.app.goo.gl/cXiR1ew7angyrpL37

Map of Padua's Best Shopping Spots

https://maps.app.goo.gl/9nmst84rN6bTMu2AA

Map of Public Transportation in Padua

https://maps.app.goo.gl/amDxiCvN1T8QLTLbA

140

Map of Parks and Gardens in Padua

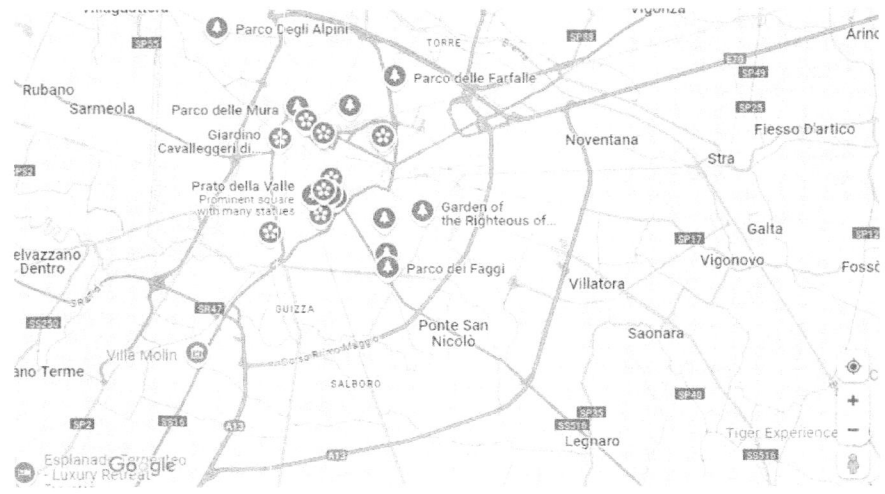

https://maps.app.goo.gl/CboGtdGAFCjsgwMD9

Thank You for Reading!

I hope you've enjoyed exploring *Padua Travel Guide 2025* and found it helpful in planning your adventure through this beautiful city.

If you found value in this guide, I'd love to hear your thoughts! A quick review would not only help me improve but also guide other travelers in discovering the wonders of Padua.

Your feedback means the world to me, and I appreciate your time and support in leaving a review.

Safe travels and happy exploring!

Warm regards,

Reed M. Callahan

Made in the USA
Las Vegas, NV
06 February 2025

17649100R00079